The Best of All Friends
'ROUND THE WREKIN

Best Wishes

Jack Insall

The Best of All Friends
'ROUND THE WREKIN

Jack Insall

ACKNOWLEDGEMENTS

There comes a time when a book is "Out of Print"
My previous four books :-
All Friends around the Wrekin.
MORE Friends around the Wrekin.
Even more Friends around the Wrekin.
You Must Be Joking.
Are now in this category, and so I have collated them into :-
THE BEST OF ALL FRIENDS 'ROUND THE WREKIN.

I could not have done this without the help of many good friends, especially Andrew Ward who took on the time consuming and detailed task of preparing the book for typesetting through his computer, and for his subsequent help in getting the book into print.

I am most grateful to Sharon Walters of the Shropshire Star and Mike Greatholder of the Telford Journal for their help, and to Livesey Ltd. for their generosity and kind co-operation.

To date generous donations towards the printing costs of £10 and over have been received from :-

Roy Batigan
Bristow and Short
Ben Van der Belt
Gill Dawes
Crown Inn (O'Gates)
Singer & Friedlander
Barclays Bank
J. Stanyer
A. Morgan
M & K Insall
MEB Ret. Members
Longmynd Travel
Cards Plus (O'Gates)
J & M Lawley
Pertemps
CG Giles (O'Gates)
Mkt. Buffet (Shrewsbury)
O'Gates Tangent Club
Hall, Butcher (O'Gates)
Telford Rag Society
Chapel of Christ the King
Kath & Pete Taylor
Dawley Baptist Sisterhood
Wrock Wood Meth. Church
Lloyds Bank
L. Tranter & Son
Marks & Spencer

Ann Scott
Homecharm (O'Gates)
David Hallam (Euro MP)
Mary Shaw
Bryan & Knott
Temperton (O'Gates)
O'Gates Carpet Co.
Muriel Murphy
ATS Midlands
Rowlands (O'Gates)
Woolworths (O'Gates)
Walford Heath Meth Ch
Just Jackie (O'Gates)
Hardy Tyres
F & G Poole
Sygnet Management
G. Leddington
Sankeys Choir Ladies
Well Evening TWG
L & O Mitton
Mrs M. S. Ward
C & S Evans
Miss B. Ferriday
Fairmile Fencing
Shropshire Newspapers
Braggs the Bakers
Eastern Generation

Magna Confectionery
Just Jackie By Design
Paul Trenberth
D. B. Roberts
S & D Cubbin
K/Bank Silver Threads
Hamilton Finance (O'Gates)
GKN Sankey Charity Trust S.
Ellerdine Methodist Chapel M
Bevelectric (O'Gates)
Rev. D. P. Smith
J. A. Harris & Sons
MG Friends Round the Wrekin
Jiva Ji (O'Gates)
Mkt. Drayton Round Table
Dentmaster
Admaston Meth Church
Prees Green Methodist Guild
R. Hatfield & G. Carlile
B'North UR & Meth Church
Mrs E. J. Holt DL
Hadley Rest Room Day Centre
New Hadley Meth. Church
O'Gates United Church
Bayston Hill Meth Discoverers
Hadley Meth Fund Raisers
The Lions Organisation

And to many friends and organisations for their generous help.

Jack Insall June 1997

"The Best of All Friends 'Round the Wrekin"
by
Jack Insall

This book, as its name implies, is a collection of monologues and stories from my previous four books.

"All Friends around the Wrekin."
"MORE Friends around the Wrekin."
"EVEN More Friends around the Wrekin."
"You Must Be Joking."

Sales of the four above-mentioned books exceeded 17,000 copies and raised over £20,000 for Charity, mostly the National Children's Home, now known as NCH Action for Children.

All of these books are now "Out of print", but I am constantly being requested to make further copies available for purchase. The obvious solution was a composite edition of the four books.

All of my Author's profits will be donated to Hope House Children's Respite Hospice.

Published by :- J.C.Insall, "Instree", Hillside Road, Ketley Bank, Telford, TF2 0BZ. Tel: 01952 612707

The Author
D.O.S.C. (NCH)

Printed by :- Livesey Ltd., Shrewsbury (01743) 235651

"The Best of All Friends 'Round the Wrekin"

"To All Friends 'round the Wrekin" is the World-famous Shropshire "Toast", which will always be associated with an old and much valued friend, the late Mr. Percy Pointon, of the Forest Glen at the foot of the Wrekin.

Copyright

ISBN 0 9506872 5 1

There can be few who have not been moved by the enthusiasm, generosity and devotion of the supporters of **"Hope House Children's Respite Hospice"** for Shropshire, Powys, Cheshire, Clwyd and Gwynedd.

And what a wonderful cause this is :-

"Hope House" is named after the Baby who inspired it, Hope Peachey from Bayston Hill who sadly died, aged 10 months.

But Hope's name lives on, and so does the inspiration which founded the Hospice.

Shirley Tart, former Women's Editor of the "Shropshire Star" and now Assistant Editor of the Express and Star has appealed to the readers to give generously to the

"Shropshire Star Hope House Special Charity".

This book is my contribution to her request for help in raising funds for this so worthy cause.

We, in this wonderful country of ours, have so much. Viscount Tonypandy, President of the National Children's Home has said that "As long as there is one child living in hardship, then we have a Christian duty to help".

I am sure that my readers will echo this sentiment and I hope, also, that they will enjoy the stories and monologues I have compiled in :-

"The BEST of All Friends 'Round the Wrekin"

Jack Insall
D.O.S.C. (NCH)

Contents

4

Contents (cont.)

What's in a Name.

The traveller said "I want to go,
to Shropshire, if you please,
by First Class train, where I can quite
relax and take my ease".

The Booking Clerk said "Thank you, Sir,
can you tell me the station,
in order that your ticket, will
be for your destination?".

"Yes Salop", said the traveller, and
the Clerk said "Ah that's Shrewsbury,
I must admit that calling Salop
Shrewsbury, does amuse me".

The traveller said "It will amuse
you more, I'm sure to learn,
That Shropshire is called Salop,
and vice versa, in its turn".

"If that's the case"the Clerk replied,
"I really fail to see,
if Salop is called Shrewsbury, how,
can Shrewsbury, Salop, be?".

"The answer to that problem", said
  the traveller,   "We are seeking,
of one thing though you can be sure,
we're All Friends Around the Wrekin".

ALW

"The Ironbridge Song"

Who doesn't know that wonderful old
tune Nellie Dean ?
Well, here's a song about that most
famous bridge of iron, at Ironbridge.

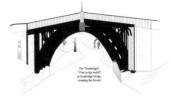

The "Ironbridge",
"First in the world",
at Ironbridge Gorge,
crossing the Severn

There's a bridge of great renown,
We esteem,   (We esteem)   *ALW*
It's the oldest in the world,
it would seem,   (It would seem)
and it stands so brave and bold,
as it did in days of old,
it is the famous old Iron Bridge,
which spans the stream.   (Which spans the stream)
If to Ironbridge by the Severn,
you have been,   (You have been)
you'll have seen this grand old bridge,
o'er the stream,   (O'er the stream)
cast and fettled in the Forge,
of the famous Severn Gorge,
where Abraham Darby, of his bridge,
would sit and dream.   (Would sit and dream)

Now from near and far they come,
they're so keen,   (they're so keen)
Her Most Gracious Majesty,
Britain's Queen,   (Britain's Queen)
so tis said, was heard to say,
"I would love to go one day,
to see this noted bridge of iron,
which spans the stream".   (which spans the stream)

"Cos I've heard about this fine
Telford scene,   (Telford scene)
and as I recall, I don't
think I've been,   (think I've been)
to this little Shropshire town,
which is now as much renowned,
as that old mill of Nellie Dean,
beside the stream".   (Sweet Nellie Dean)

THE WREKIN TOAST

From John O' Groats to far Lands End,
Each County and location,
Was obviously favoured by the,
Lord in his creation.

The Cornishman, as we all know,
Is such a spendid fellow,
Who'll sing the famous Floral dance,
From Penzance to Polperro.

Whilst Devon, Glorious Devon,
Boasts the well known Plymouth Hoe,
From which we're told, Sir Francis Drake,
Was very loth to go.

In Somerset, the cider apples,
Grow upon the trees,
Whilst who could ask for more,
Than Weston Super Mare's sea breeze.

In Yorkshire they're a canny lot,
Especially with the bat,
But do beware what can befall,
On Ilkley Moor, bah't hat.

In Oxfordshire their very proud,
Of Banbury and its Cross,
At Coventry, in Warwickshire,
Godiva on her hoss.

The oyster beds at Whitstable,
The sights of London Town,
The Dunmow Flitch, the Worcester
Sauce,
And china of renown.

ALW

These are but just a very few,
Which merit some attention,
And which the guide book probably,
Will p'raps seem to mention.

8

But there's a County, much beloved,
whose Sons and Daughters share,
where'er they be throughout the world,
a bond of friendship rare.

It is the famous Shropshire toast,
"To all friends round the Wrekin,
and to Her Most Royal Majesty,
the loyalty she is seeking".

"To Shropshire's Sons upon the sea,
 on land and in the air,
there never were, nor ever will,
be finer, anywhere".

ALW

"For they have never bowed the knee,
in bondage, to a foe,
nor ever will, while they have breath,
to fight as best they know".

"And may the Good Lord please rain down,
upon our foes' bare shins,
as many Holy pebble stones,
as they've committed sins".

"In order that we'll know them,
by the way they cringe and crimp,
but more especially, so we'll know,
the *blighters* by their limp".

"To All Friends 'Round the Wrekin" .

*   *   *   *   *

"The Tollgate"
A Tale of Ironbridge

ON that famous old bridge o'er the Severn,
at Ironbridge, as everyone knows,
there once was a full working Toll-gate,
while Toll-house was sited quite close.

If thee wantedst to make a quick journey,
from Ironbridge to Broseley, or back,
the Toll thee would'st pay at the Toll-gate,
to keep Toll-gate Trust in the black.

Near the gate in his house, stood Toll-keeper,
a famous old character, he,
most civil, polite, and obliging,
providing thee payest thee fee.

He rejoiced in the good name of Enoch,
a Shropshire Mon true, born and bred,
as a rule he would stand in his doorway,
but sometimes he'd sit down, instead.

ALW

As thee comes't to the gate, he would greet thee,
with "Now my Mon, what's it to be,
a one day return for a penny,
or a single for one ha-penny?".

If thee wantedst to go to the Station,
Owd Enoch would ask thee straight out,
"Bist going to Bridgnorth or Salop?,
be back for thee tea, I've no doubt".

As a rule it were humdrum existence,
for Enoch, just standing about,
but every so often his bête-noir appeared,
in the form of Owd Sam, the town lout.

Owd Sam liked to gently bait Enoch,
by saying he weren't going to pay,
and to make matters worse, he'd pull out his purse,
and then quickly put it away.

Now Enoch at first tried to reason,
with "Look Sam, let's talk this thing out,
supposing our roles were reversed now,
and things were t'other way 'bout".

"If thee wast to ask me for toll-fee,
I'd give it to thee like a shot",
but Sam said "Ah, that's where theet wrong then,
cos I amma thee, and theese not".

Owd Enoch could see he were beaten,
and then he said, most carefully,
"Did I understand thee correctly,
dids't thee say *ONE* prisoner was free?"

"Thats right", said the bobby, "Thee heards't me,
thee asna got cloth ears, I trust",
at which Enoch suddenly bridled,
and knocked Bobby's hat in the dust.

"Hey, what's going on?", said the Bobby,
"Thee cosna Knock off policeman's hat,
it just isn't done , especially for fun,
I'll have to arrest thee for that".

"Exactly, my Mon", said Owd Enoch,
"And quoting thy Sub-Section "C",
as theese landed thyself with *two* prisoners,
thee wouldna be having one free".

"Including thyself, that's three ha-pence,
I assume that we're going one way,
cos it's ha-penny a time for a single,
or a penny return for same day".

*   *   *   *   *

"Ironbridge and Broseley"
A Tale of The Severn Valley Line

FROM Bewdley to Shrewsbury the line ran,
through Bridgnorth and Highley, and on,
through Coalport and Jackfield to Ironbridge and Broseley,
a station which sadly has gone.

From the lives of so many who knew it,
and how in it's finest heyday,
was the pride of the whole Severn Valley,
and probably is to this day.

What a thrill as the once mighty engines,
came steaming in on the "Up" line,
and being "The Great Western Railway",
you could well set your watch by their time.

If travelling to Wenlock, the porter would shout,
"Change at Buildwas, don't travel straight through,
for Coalbrookdale, Wellington, Stafford and Crewe,
make sure that you're on Platform Two".

The Staff were the finest you ever did see,
from Gaffer to youngest trainee,
The whole place abounded with vigour and joy,
and unequalled efficiency.

To the valleys of Wales, six waggons a day,
were dispatched along permanent way,
and what were they loaded with?, Well to be sure,
Miner's pipes made from pure Broseley clay.

While just down at Jackfield, the tileries there,
were making best tiles in the land,
Famous firms such as Maws, Craven Dunhills, and such,
were hard put to fill World demand.

The passenger traffic was steady and good,
Commuters used Railway each day,
some travelled to Bridgnorth or Shrewsbury and back,
while some only travelled half-way.

A cheap Day Excursion to Shrewsbury, return,
cost ninepence, or was it a bob?,
if you travelled First Class, then you paid a bit more,
and were thought just a bit of a snob.,

As a rule it were peaceful as peaceful could be,
with trains coming in on the hour,
but just once a year on Eyton Race day,
the system would suddenly sour.

For first race would always start well before two,
but thousands would come at last minute,
to get on the train if they possibly could,
and stretch the poor staff to the limit

"Tell Sid"

Communication has been practised,
since the world began,
with messages scrawled in the sand,
by prehistoric man.

One such, discovered recently,
read, "If thou see'est Sid,
remember to remind him, that,
he oweth me a quid".

Another one, quite close at hand,
read, "Don't forget to tell,
young Master Sid, about his folks,
who all are keeping well".

And then to cap it all, writ on,
a cliff face, steep and sheer,
the message read, "Tell Sidney, please,
that Kilroy has been here".

But latterly, of course we hear,
a lot about young Sid,
who's canvassing the British Race,
To cough up fifty quid.

Who knows?, when we pass over,
will St. Peter standing there,
say, "Look at Sid, disconsolate,
without a single share".

Because nobody told the lad,
he missed his opening bid,
so please, in future, don't forget,
What 'ere you do, TELL SID".

Half a Swede

A great big man entered a shop,
and said to the assistant,
"I want to purchase half a swede,
and eat it now this instant".

The Sales Assistant, who was small,
replied "This can't be done,
we don't cut swedes in half, you see,
for you or anyone".

The big man said "Then watch my lips,
I'm wanting half a swede",
The Sales Assistant said "To your
request I can't accede".

"The swedes are sold as they're displayed,
and can't be cut in two",
I'm very sorry, Sir, but that's
the best that I can do".

The big man now moved closer
to the small assistant, who,
retreated to the office, where
his boss was working, too.

The Sales Assistant said "Look Boss,
your help I really need,
the biggest ugliest man I've seen,
is wanting half a swede".

The big man in the doorway stood,
The small man with a laugh,
said Boss "And this kind gentleman,
will buy the other half".

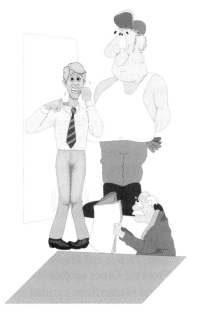

ALW

"If thee'st called before me", said owd Enoch,
"Wut promise me, Sam, theet come down,
and tell me what happens up yonder,
and whether the green's flat or crown?".

"While I, for my part, promise thee, Sam,
if I go before thee, I'll swear,
to return when I can to inform thee,
what brew thee should'st ask for, up there".

Thus, now that there future was settled,
they really had only one aim,
to play bowls from morning to evening,
enjoying this wonderful game.

By something far stranger than fiction,
coincidence p'raps, if you will,
twere only a week a two later,
that Enoch were taken quite ill.

Twere said he'd got chill from his bowling,
and walking across the wet grass,
while others said Enoch had caught it,
by supping out of a damp glass.

Before Enoch died, he said, "Samuel,
thee knowest what I vowed unto thee,
I haven't forgotten me promise,
I'll come back as soon as I'm free".

"So just thee keep on with thee bowling,
and drinking me health, while thee cost,
Drink to the games that we've won, Sam,
and also to those that we've lost".

"And now as I make me last journey,
where millions of others have been,
remember, me, Sam, when theese bowling,
on't Nabb on the Bird in Hand Green".

So saying Owd Enoch departed,
and Sam, for a partner, looked round,
but though one or two seemed quite friendly,
they wunna like Enoch, he found,

Then one day as Samuel were sittting,
on't bench, near the green, at The Bird,
a voice said, "Sam Lad, it's me, Enoch,
I promised thee, I'd keep me word".

"I canna stop long, but I'll tell thee,
there's good news and bad news to tell,
I'm in Paradise, Sam, so they tell me,
which is somewhere twixt Heaven and Hell".

"Lor, Bless my Soul", said Owd Samuel,
"I knew theet not end up below,
hast got any time for thee bowling,
are greens any good, wut thee know?".

ALW

"Theese never seen bowling greens like em",
said Enoch, "The grass is so green,
and smooth as a young baby's bottom,
with never a rut to be seen".

"As theeese never been up here theeself, Sam,
thee wutna believe what I say,
but all thee owd mates round the Wrekin,
are playing on't greens, every day"

"And just afore I come to see thee
and hoping I shouldn't be missed,
the bad news for thee, Sam, I noticed,
was thy name was clearly on't list".

"For a match to be played off, tomorrow,
when again theel't be partnering me,
Come to think ont, these looking quite pale, Sam,
if theese quick, thee could'st come back with me".

"Thee go on", said Owd Samuel, "I'll follow",
and giving Owd Enoch a wink,
Sam pushed his pint mug o'er the counter,
and ordered his very last drink.

Before joining up with Owd Enoch,
To play in that wonderful land,
with all his owd mates round the Wrekin,
who'd played at the Nabb, Bird in Hand.

ALW

The action swung from end to end,
first Wolves and then the Town,
strove might and main to get the goal,
which would their efforts crown.

Until young Billy Rafferty,
gave Wolves the vital lead,
or so they thought, until Maguire,
put on a turn of speed.

Which left the full-back standing,
while Pete Daniel blocked his view,
and stopped Maguire from scoring,
in the only way he knew.

The Ref., a Welshman of of repute,
just pointed to the spot,
where Atkins beat the goalie,
with a mighty powerful shot.

The die was cast, the game was drawn,
the fans went on their way,
for Wolves a disappointment, but,
for Town, a great replay.

SPORTS SPECIAL
EXTRA
SHREWSBURY TOWN
CHAMPIONS
OF
DIVISION THREE

ALW

Which took place at the Meadow, and,
though Town fought valiantly,
they only found the net but once,
while Wanderers scored three.

Thus shall they be immortalised,
the team from Shrewsbury Town,
who kept on fighting to the end,
although they were three down.

And proved the saying once again,
"It's not what's in a name",
but as these proud Salopians shewed,
"The way you play the game".

They knew not then, as we know now,
their finest hour would be,
when they became the Champions,
of League Division Three.

Whilst on holiday in the summer of 1988, a charming lady, Mrs. Waterworth of Salford, suggested that many of my readers would enjoy this little monologue. And so with acknowledgement to it's Author.

"Memories"

We met and were married a long time ago,
And worked for long hours when the wages were low.

No TV. No wireless, no bath, times were hard,
Just a cold water tap, and a loo in the yard.

No going abroad, and no carpets on floors,
We had coal on the fire, and we didn't lock doors.

Our children arrived as a gift from the Lord,
And were brought up as Christians, to live by His word.

They were safe going, out and could play in the park,
Whilst the old folks could go for a walk in the dark.

No Valium, no drugs, nor what's called LSD.,
We cured most of our ills with a good cup of tea..

No vandals, no muggings, with nothing to to rob,
We felt we were rich with a couple of bob.

And people were happy in those far off days,
Much kinder and caring in so many ways.

While milkmen and tradesmen would whistle and sing,
A night at the pictures was "Doing our thing".

We all get our fair share of troubles and strife,
And just have to face up to that part of life.

But now I'm alone, I look back through the years,
Forgetting the bad times, the trouble and tears.

Rememb'ring the blessings, our home and our love,
Which we shared as a family — I thank God above.

And hope that my children, and their children, too,
Will remember the memories, that I've shared with you.

"I'll try another day"

When King Canute rebuked the waves,
He thought that he would be,
the only person in the world,
who could turn back the sea.

But very soon he realized,
the waves would not obey,
and so he thought, "I'll give this up,
and try another day".

King Alfred, when he burnt the cakes,
Was overheard to say,
"Well, anyone can get it wrong,
I'll try another day".

Whilst 'Enery the Eighth could claim,
in all sincerity,
beheading his beloved wives,
was done too hastily.

For once he'd had them "topped", there was,
no way that he could say,
"I think I've changed me mind, me Dear
I'll try another day".

And Cromwell, searching round the famous,
Oak at Boscobel.
was unaware that Charles was up the,
tree, alive and well.

Just quietly singing to himself,
that well known roundelay,
"If firstly I do not succeed,
I'll try another day" .

'Tis even said, Victoria,
in all her majesty,
was not amused, when Gladstone said,
"We'll have to wait and see".

"Be good enough, kind Sir", Quoth she,
"With dalliance do away,
It is our wish, you'll answer thus,
I'll try another day".

So, through the ages, Kings and Queens,
and famous people too,
have proved that they can make mistakes,
the same as me and you.

As Hansard will no doubt record,
the question we must beg,
was poor Edwina Curry right,
or wrong, about the egg?.

And is it p'raps just possible,
she nightly kneels to pray,
"Please give me one more chance, that I,
can try another day".

For boiled or scrambled, poached or fried,
this must at least be said,
the British egg will always be,
"The best thing since Sliced Bread".

ALW

"The Granville"
An East Shropshire Mining Tale

ON the road from St. Georges to Cannock,
in a meadow, just off the Red Hill,
there once lived a most famous gardener,
who went by the name of 'Owd Bill'.

Now Bill used to sit in his garden,
or more often lean on his spade,
and think of the wondrous creation,
the Good Lord he worshipped had made.

So proud was Owd Bill of his garden,
he wouldn't let anyone in,
unless they had made an appointment,
except for his own kith and kin.

Now next to Owd Bill lived Owd Enoch,
who didn't did think much of Owd Bill,
and as Bill thought little of Enoch,
there wasn't a lot of goodwill.

Cos Enoch thought nothing of gardening,
he did all his digging each day,
in the bowels of the earth under Madeley,
for little, or very poor pay.

This state of things couldn't continue,
for Miners and such, and the like,
and so they had Countrywide meetings,
to start a big Countrywide strike.

ALW

T'were a strike that soon paralysed Nation,
cos nobody had any fuel,
and none missed it more than Owd Enoch,
who felt the cold winds something cruel.

So being an underground worker,
and well used to using his head,
he looked out with pride at his garden,
and then with a knowing look said.

"If there's clay on the top of the sub-soil,
and Penistone Rock just below,
there's got to be coal down there somewhere,
as any good miner should know".

So getting his pick and his shovel,
he started to dig a big hole,
and ere very long had soon struck it,
a seam of the very best coal.

He dug and he picked and he shovelled,
by morning, by noon, and by night,
his tunnel grew longer and longer,
and disappeared right out of sight.

Owd Bill, in the meantime was gardening,
his lawn was a joy to behold,
It was just like a lovely green carpet,
so straight, and so smooth, and well rolled.

As he stood with his mower in the middle,
he couldn't believe his old eyes,
a dirty big hole was appearing,
and just to complete his surprise.

Owd Enoch appeared with a shovel,
all blackfaced and covered with coal,
Owd Bill thought that he were the devil,
come back in the shape of a mole.

Now Enoch were so busy digging,
he didn't see Bill standing there,
so throwing the coal o'er his shoulder,
he caught poor Owd Bill fair and square.

As if from a dream Bill awakened,
and realised what was afoot,
and then he made straight for Owd Enoch,
and started to put in the boot.

Owd Enoch fought back like a good un,
and dragged Owd Bill down into hole,
where both of them rolled to the bottom,
all covered with finest grade coal.

The Best Remedy

Owd Sam had a terrible cough,
so Elsie, his wife, said to Sam,
"Thee get theeself down to the Doctor,
and get there as fast as thee can".

When Samuel returned from the Doctor,
Elsie said to him "What did he say,
Did he give you some linctus and balsam,
to take three or four times a day?".

Owd Samuel said "No Else, he didna,
He towd me to take straight away,
Epsom Salts in a glass of hot water,
and Syrup of Figs in me tay".

"Liquid Paraffin too, would be useful,
to be taken 'ere going to bed",
"Now I'm sure if you take my advice, Sam,
You'll be fit as a fiddle", he said.

"Will this stop me coughing then, Doctor?",
"It certainly will Sam, instead,
You'll be far too afraid to start coughing,
It's the best cure I know of" he said.

ALW

"Signalman Charlie's Pigeon"

*A true tale, well almost, of the G.W.R. With grateful acknowledgement
to my friend Stan Burgess, Ex G.W.R. driver (Now retired).*

In the days of the Great Western Railway,
fondly known as the G.W.R.,
all the staff were good friends with each other,
and to this day, they probably are.

Every signalman knew all the drivers,
and the stokers, who passed by each day,
as well as the shunters and gangers,
who worked on the permanent way.

They were just like a big happy family,
and so, when a favour was sought,
they'd go out of their way, to ensure no delay,
was encountered before this was wrought.

Thus it happened that Enoch, the driver,
and Samuel, his stoker and mate,
were requested by signalman Charlie,
to carry some valuable freight.

In the shape of Owd Charlie's prize pigeon,
to a station, ten miles down the line,
and release him as soon as they got there,
so Charlie could check the bird's time

Well, the pigeon was taken from Charlie,
and the signal was set to "All Clear",
"Don't forget" said Owd Charlie, "To free him,
I'll expect him in no time, back here".

On a day's outing to Bath, I found this little story in a Christian Bookshop.
I couuldn't resist the challenge of putting it into verse, as a monologue.

"The Pilgrim's Cross"

A Pilgrim, bent low, 'neath the weight of his Cross,
Saw a hewer of wood, felling trees,
"I wonder kind Sir", said the man of the Cloth,
"If a favour you'd do for me please?".

"Why certainly Brother", the woodman replied,
"If you'll just tell me what I can do,
I'll do it at once, and with pleasure, I'm sure,
free of charge, for a Pilgrim, like you".

"My Cross is so heavy, to carry so far",
Said the Pilgrim, "Along the hard road,
If you'll chop an inch off or two, I'll be obliged,
For I'm sure it will lighten my load".

The woodman soon shortened the Cross, with his axe,
and the Pilgrim set off on his way,
unaware of the pitfalls that lay in his path,
and the price he would now have to pay.

For directly in front of him, guarding the Gates,
of the Kingdom, there stood a divide,
A chasm as deep as the deepest sea bed,
so deep, and so long, and so wide.

"My Cross", thought the Pilgrim, "I'll use as a bridge,
for it's strong, though it's simple and rough",
But he found when he tried, that it just wouldn't reach,
by exactly the length he'd cut off.

'Twas then that the Pilgrim awoke from his dream,
and vowed that he never again,
would lighten his Cross, on his journey through life,
to establish a temporary gain.

From that moment on, through his Faith in the Lord,
He discovered his Cross, day by day,
was lighter to carry, with each step he took,
to the end of his Pilgrimage Way.

"The Forest Glen"

When first the Forest Glen was built,
t'was little thought, one day,
that it would be dismantled, and,
erected, far away.

From where it's been these many years,
below that famous hill,
which stands so proudly on the plain,
and no doubt always will.

For many thousands, having climbed,
The Wrekin, would repair,
without delay, straight to The Glen,
to partake of it's fare.

Of lemonade and cups of tea,
and sandwichs and buns,
and ice-cream cornets, loved by all,
the children and their Mums.

Whilst every night, or so it seemed,
The Annual Dinner Dance,
for many Clubs, both far and near,
would 'ere afford the chance.

For Percy Pointon to appear,
The Forest Glen's Mine Host,
to render in immortal style,
The famous Wrekin Toast.

Which calls upon Salopians proud,
to raise their glasses high,
To all brave Shropshire Lads who fought,
on land, or sea, or sky.

To Britain's Queen, long may she reign,
and always be assured,
of Shropshire's loyalty to the Crown,
so constantly averred.

And to the Lord, a plea, sincere,
for pebblestones to rain,
upon our foes' bare shins, so that,
we'll know them, once again.

For though they think we know them not,
because they cringe and crimp,
there is no doubt, we'll recognise,
The BLIGHTERS, by their limp.

And so the dear old Forest Glen,
restored and well preserved,
will keep alive the memories,
to which it's purpose served.

For now, in very truth, it has,
been rebuilt at Blists Hill,
where, as of old, the welcome cuppa,
Can be savoured, still.

The Ironbridge Gorge Museum Trust,
of one thing can be sure,
The famous Shropshire Wrekin Toast,
for all the time will endure.

Because for all Salopians, proud,
whenever they are speaking,
for evermore the toast will be,
"To All Friends Round the Wrekin"

"Floreat Salopia"

'Tis said there lived in Shrewsbury Town,
a long, long, time ago,
A man whose vision brought about,
The famous Floral Show.

It seems, whilst walking in the fields,
down by the riverside,
He visualised a Flower Show Ground,
the world would eye with pride.

A place for all to saunter in,
without a care or worry,
The lovely parkland by the Severn,
we now know as,......"The Quarry".

And then he thought, "We'll need a place,
where one and all can mingle,
in quite reflection, midst the flowers",
and so he built,...... "The Dingle".

A haven in a bustling world,
of peace and tranquil, rare,
Created for the likes of all,
who would God's beauty share.

A place where all Salopians,
can find the joy they're seeking,
in company with all their friends,
"Who live around the Wrekin".

ALW

A Supermarket Tale

A Supermarket Manager,
was beaming with delight,
The store was full of shoppers,
buying everything in sight.

He thought if this goes on I'm sure
promoted I shall be,
to manage a much larger store,
in some locality".

And then from near a checkout, came
a loud and plaintive cry,
"Stop thief, Stop thief, you've robbed me of
me steak and kidney pie".

The Manager then called the police,
who very quickly came,
to find out who the culprit was,
and apprehend the same.

The customer, a poor old man,
had by this time relaxed,
and so, when questioned by the police,
was sure about his facts.

He said "The robbers hit me hard,
upon me back, and head,
They hit me with a bag of spuds,
it's lucky I'm not dead".

"And would you recognise them, sir,
if you saw them again?",
"Of course I've grown 'em all me life,
King Edwards is their name".

ALW

"Fudge"
The Shrewsbury Watch-Dog

I don't suppose we'll ever know,
or guess the reason why,
The lady in the nursery rhyme,
consumed a little fly.

Which, followed by a spider,
to digest that little fly,
was fair enough, but still 'twas thought,
the dear old soul would die.

Nor can we fail to be amazed,
at that most glorious tale,
of how young Jonah fared inside,
the belly of a whale.

But here's a story strange, but true,
of how Glenn Miller's swing,
compelled a Shrewsbury Boxer Dog,
to try and do his thing.

It seems, his Master's favourite watch,
was nowhere to be found,
and yet where're the Boxer went,
one still could hear the sound.

Of Glenn's "American Patrol",
played with the Maestro's power
and coming through, quite clear and loud,
exactly on the hour.

In every cranny, every nook,
again and yet again,
the family searched with all their might,
Alas, it was in vain.

In fact, it could be fairly said,
"They hunted here and there,
they hunted high, they hunted low,
and searched most everywhere".

Until the laddie of the house,
said "Dad, the watch is found,
it's in the tummy of young fudge,
our music - loving hound".

Who much prefers a tasty watch,
to usual doggy food,
especially with Glenn Miller's Band,
to get him in the mood.

And so indeed, it proved to be,
the watch was in the dog,
whose fame had spread both far and wide,
with all the world agog.

Just wondering how the dog would fare,
and which would be the day,
when Fudge the Boxer, famous now,
would pass the time away.

ALW

The Photograph

Young Sam was looking at his Dad's
old photograph, he'd found,
and thought he'd like a copy made
that he could show around.

So, as he passed Boots Chemist Shop,
where photos are processed,
He thought "This is the place to come,
I'am sure they'll do their best".

He asked a kind assistant if
a copy could be done,
of his old Father's photograph,
She said "Of course my Son".

And then he said "I wonder if
it's possible to take
my Father's hat off in the one
that you are going to make?".

The kind assistant said "It is
a process we're just starting,
The only thing we need to know,
in which side was his parting?".

Young Sam appeared to be nonplussed,
and said "Well fancy that,
You'll see which side his parting was
when you remove his hat".

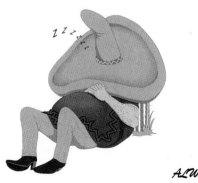

ALW

In August, 1980 I received this letter from Mr. C. R. Moore of Madeley.
Dear Mr. Insall,
I have been reading your book "All Friends Around the Wrekin", which I have enjoyed very much. I thought you might be interested in the enclosed monologue, written in 1936 about Madelely Old Folk's Rest Room.
Two points of explanation may be useful. The line "Uncle brings 'em in with the bread", refers to the founder of the Rest Room, R. N. Moore, known to everybody as "Uncle Bob", and who had a bakery business in Madeley.
The very last line "And women", refers to the fact that the Rest Room welcomed both men and women, whereas nearly all of the few O. A. P.'s Clubs of that time, were for men only.
I hope you find this an interesting addition to your collection of Shropshire monologues.
Yours sincerely,
C. R. Moore.

"Sam visits the Rest Room at Madeley"

(With apologies to Stanley Holloway). By Mr. W. E. Moore of Sheffield.

Sam were cleaning up his musket,
wot'e fired at Waterloo,
W'en daft like 'e tipped up basin,
wot wer full of Irish stew,
Now on bottom o' this basin,
there were "coalport" printed plain,
Wanderin' spirit took our hero,
and he said "I'm off to train",
So 'e 'ops it to the station,
and 'e says to ticket man,
"Give me there and back to Coalport,
Seein' basins made's my plan".

Sam 'e landed safe at Coalport,
and 'e walked 'him round and round,
but in spite of all his efforts,
China works weren't to be found,
Then 'e spots a local woman,
Says "if I might trouble you,
could you show me works at Coalport,
wot made basin for my stew?"
Woman looked at Sam old-fashioned,
Then she said "Thee'st very queer;
dost thee know that China factory
hast been moved for many a year?".

Then Old Sam said "More's the pity,
that I came , an didn't know,
but I've spent a pile o' money,
hast thou nothing else to shew"
Smilingly, she said to Samuel,
"Now I'll shew thee a new trick",
So she took him up to Madeley,
To a building made o' brick,
Place were full o' aged people,
and they wore a happy smile,
Who said old uns can't be happy?,
Rest Room makes their life worthwhile.

Woman said "It's grand on Fridays:
Speakers come from far and near,
Singers, Players, and Reciters
Bring their messages of cheer;
Every Birthday is remembered,
Them wot finds it hard to tread,
Bless your heart, they're not forgotten:
Uncle brings em with the bread".

Then she said how sick and dyin'
Found a friend when needed most,
Could Sam wonder for a moment,
That such work made old uns boast?.
Sam had never heard such singin',
Children of three score and over
Chanted out "I am so happy",
He could see they were in clover,
When the meeting were concluded'
people crowded round the table,
Parson signed their pension papers,
helps in every way he's able.

Sam, he cried, he was so happy,
and upon his journey home,
told himself he'd move to Madeley,
livin' peaceful, ne'er to roam,
You who've been inside the Rest Room
know it's worth. You'll come again,
You who havn't, visit Madeley,
Home of happy aged men,
* * * * * AND WOMEN * * * * *

And in those far off days, as now,
for quite a modest fee,
T'was possible to rest one's legs,
and have a cup of tea.

Now thus refreshed, the Giant said,
"The gold that I am seeking,
I'll dig out here, right where I stand",
and so, he built the Wrekin.

A tidy man, when work was done,
He liked his shoes to sparkle,
so on his spade, he cleaned his boots,
which thus became the......Ercall.

* * * *

"The Gardener"

When Adam sinned in Eden fair,
by eating of the apple,
'Tis thought, the Good Lord wondered if,
the lad was adaptable,

And if provided with a spade,
to dig the goodly earth,
It surely would not take too long,
to ascertain his worth.

Thus, as Eve spun and Adam toiled,
to earn their Maker's pardon,
although they hadn't realised,
they'd made the World's first garden,

Since when, it has been evident,
through every generation,
A garden makes a man grow up,
in his own estimation.

ALW

He'll talk for hours about his flowers,
just like a modern Moses,
and woe betide the simple soul,
Who praises up his roses.

For now he's got you on the spot,
about his floribundas,
You'll find the darned things grow on you,
like one of Nature's wonders.

He'll show you round the cabbages,
and as for his best marrow,
Lord help the man who has to load,
that thing onto a barrow.

On fertilisers he'll enthuse,
His knowledge is terrific,
which on a fine warm summer's day,
can be quite soporific.

And this where your gardener, will,
with true Salopian guile,
prove to himself, yet once again,
that gardening's so worthwhile.

In some secluded favourite spot,
He'll light his old briar pipe,
and dream of his tomatoes, which,
He'll gather when they're ripe.

A millionaire could not achieve,
the peace of mind he'll know,
that having sown the goodly seed,
The Lord will make it grow.

ALW

*   *   *   *

"A Shropshire Lass"

When Housman wrote "A Shropshire Lad",
a Shropshire Lass would know,
instinctively, the time and the place,
to capture her young beau.

A flutter of an eyelid, or,
a kerchief on the ground,
would be enough, she knew full well,
to bring the boys around,

For Shropshire Lads, like Raleigh, when,
his cloak he laid for Bess,
would to themselves be true, to help,
a damsel in distress..

And should a lady board a train,
her search to find a seat,
would certainly be very short,
And very, very sweet.

For every seated gentleman,
would rise with "If you please,
I would be most obliged if you
will sit and take your ease".

On Sunday evenings after Church,
each Shropshire Lass would know,
a favourite walk, where she knew well,
she'd meet young, "So and so".

Who'd doff his cap, politely bow,
and ask if he might be,
an escort for the Lady fair,
to keep her company.

To which the comely Shropshire Lass,
would graciously assent,
because she knew the Shropshire Lad's
intentions were well meant.

ALW

His chivalry and manners fair,
were quite, she felt, Utopian,
and furthermore , he was of course,
a very Proud Salopian.

He was, in fact, the Shropshire Lad,
a Shropshire Lass was seeking,
to wed, and raise a family of
All Friends Around the Wrekin.

On the Promenade

Sam and Elsie loved to spend
a few days by the sea,
where they could rest their weary limbs,
and so contented be.

They'd been to Weston Super Mare,
to Colwyn Bay and Rhyl,
but there was one resort, they felt,
would always fill the bill.

And that was breezy Blackpool, with
it's sun and sea and sand,
It's wondrous Tower and Pleasure Beach,
the finest in the land.

One day, whilst on the promenade,
where Sam and Elsie sat,
a seagull that was taken short,
marked Elsie's favourite hat.

"Do something quickly, Sam" she cried,
in obvious distress,
for there's no doubt her titfer was
in something of a mess.

"Please get some paper, Sam at once,
or there will be a row",
"Don't be so daft" Sam said "That bird
is miles away by now".

ALW

"Paradise"

St.Peter, standing by the gates,
of Paradise, one day,
was asking people in the queue,
how they would like to pay.

"A cheque book is no good", said he,
"Up here we don't need money,
because The Promised Land o'erflows,
with lots of milk and honey".

"An Access or a BarclayCard
is also to be spurned,
because your only credit, is,
for what on Earth you've earned".

"The stocks and Shares you bought and sold,
and all those shrewd investments,
will not, I fear, while you're up here,
afford you much contentment.

At which, a Shropshire Lass spoke up,
and said, "That's good advice,
but tell us, Sir, how can we then,
get into Paradise?".

"We've only brought out of the World
our name and reputation",
St. Peter smiled, and gently said,
"There is one consolation".

"If, on the Earth, you helped someone,
along life's weary way,
You can be sure your kindly deed,
was entered up each day".

"Recorded, in the Book of Life,
the time, and place,and dates,
That is the way, my friend, you'll pay,
to pass these Pearly Gates".

ALW

"A Nursery Quiz"

It is a very well known fact,
that we can all recall,
the nursery rhymes we loved to hear,
when we were very small.

But now we're older, it would seem,
a good idea to find,
the reason why these little rhymes,
amused our childish minds,

Why Willie Winkie, clad it seems,
In just a thin nightgown,
would spend the evenings, so we're told,
in scampering round the town?

Or why Jack Sprat could eat no fat,
and licked the platter clean,
to help his wife make sure, she,
wasn't left with all the lean.

Or why Miss Moffet loved to eat
her dish of curds and whey,
until that nasty spider, chased,
the little girl away?.

And why young Polly Flinders, should,
among the cinders sit?,
is very hard to understand,
and well beyond our wit.

While Humpty Dumpty never should,
have climbed upon that wall,
which caused him all those injuries,
in such a dreadful fall.

ALW

One cannot but feel sorry for
the Woman in the Shoe,
who had so many children that
She knew not what to do.

Today, of course, the Welfare State,
would help in every way,
in Family Planning matters, and ,
her bills and such to pay.

And thinking of the Crooked Man,
who ran a crooked mile,
He'd never bother now, to seek,
that sixpence by the stile.

Nor would the Grand Old Duke of York,
and his ten thousand men,
be so inclined to scale that hill,
and march them down again.

Because in 1997,
The unions would say,
"Come on now Lads, We'll knock off work,
unless we get more pay".

And Mother Hubbard never would,
go searching for a bone,
with all the doggy food in tins,
that she could carry home.

Goosey Gander, Simple Simon,
Bo Peep and her sheep,
were often Mother's last resort,
to get us off to sleep.

But still the question haunts me why,
those youngsters, Jack and Jill,
complete with pail,would want to scale,
and clamber up that hill.

Is it perhaps more likely that,
with adolescent sparkle,
Young Jack and Jill, as couples will,
were snogging on the Ercall!

And took the little pail along
with them, as good intent,
to thus confuse the onlookers,
and throw them off the scent.

But why did Jill come tumbling down,
and why did Jack come after?,
could it , perhaps, because they both
were so convulsed with laughter!

At thinking how, in years to come,
so many would be speaking,
of how they went to fetch a pail,
of water, up the Wrekin.

For there's no doubt, on looking back,
this was that famous hill,
beloved of countless children, in,
the tale of Jack and Jill.

A hill whose fame is such, that o'er,
the world, when folk are speaking,
of Jack and Jill, they're thinking of,
"All Friends Around the Wrekin".

ALW

Some kind friend sent me the following,
which I understand, is the original famous Shropshire Toast.

"All Friends Around the Wrekin"

There never blows a strong wind,
On Stiperstones or Long Mynd,
Fair is the face of summer morning,
Over the hills of Clee;
Caradoc tells of old renown,
Haughmond smiles on Shrewsbury Town,
But the joy and pride of Severnside,
Is the Wrekin crowned in majesty,
Floreat Salopia.

Then Here's to All Friends round the Wrekin,
Let honour be paid to the toast;
There's no other Shire,
A sentiment prouder than Shropshire can boast,
"All Friends Round the Wrekin".

On fertile plain and hillside,
By river, mere and rillside,
Nature weaves her magic smile anew,
From day to day,
Lambkins o'er the meadows bound,
Woodlands wake to horse and hound,
All cares take wing, where peace reigns kind,
And friendship tunes a roundelay.

Our share in England's glory,
Is famed in song and story;
Clive and Hill and Benbow.
All are living memories yet;
Long as ever Severn runs,
Shropshire counts her gallant sons;
The world still reads of doughty deeds,
That Britons never will forget.

W. Herbert Scott

I am grateful for the opportunity of including these treasured lines in this book
of Salopiana.   The Author

The Birthday

An Englishman, an Irishman,
A Scotsman and a Taff,
were trying to outdo each other,
just to get a laugh.

The Englishman said "I've a boy
born whilst I was away,
and christened George because he came
on good St. George's day".

The Scotsman said "Well, fancy that,
I too was far away,
when our son Andrew came along,
on good St. Andrew's day".

The Welshman said "To follow that
I don't know what to say,
because our David, too, was born
on good St. David's day".

The Irishman said "Though our Patron
Saint is good St. Patrick,
it would appear to me, you three
have really scored a hat trick".

"Our son came on Shrove Tuesday, thus
the choice we had to make,
was somewhat limited, and so,
we christened him PANCAKE".

ALW

"A Japanese Toast"

In olden days, or so we're told,
it was quite often said,
"That Shropshire folk were strong in th'arm,
But very weak in th'ead".

This is, of course, an old wives' tale,
as all the world can tell,
that Shropshire folk, are strong in th'arm,
and strong in th'ead as well.

Which is, no doubt, the reason why,
Firms from the Rising Sun,
have set up home and place of work,
In Telford's Wellington.

In fact, there is a rumour
The Mikado of Japan,
would like to be the M.P. for
The Wrekin, if he can.

One surely can envisage, if,
this trend goes on and on,
The Shropshire town of "Titipu",
instead of "Wellington".

And Shropshire's famous toast will be,
translated thus, in speaking,
In Saki, we will dlink the health of,
"All Fliends Lound the Lekin".

ALW

"Neighbouring Wolverhampton"

As far back as I can remember,
which goes back a very long way,
I've always enjoyed Wolverhampton,
when coming to Town, for the day.

In the old days, the Low Level Station,
was where we all got off the train,
In the days of the Great Western Railway,
which sadly we'll ne'er see again.

Then up through the Town we would wander,
past the Grand, with it's great pantomime,
and the many fine shows they put on there,
especially around Christmas time.

Round Woolies, and Marks, and through Beatties,
we'd do all our shopping, and then,
have a hot buttered roll and a cuppa,
before going back home again.

But now there's the new Mander Centre,
of which Wolverhampton can say,
There's no better place in the Midlands,
to spend an enjoyable day.

With the single exception of Telford,
It's only a few miles away,
with shops you'll adore, and car parks galore,
and nothing, yes nothing, to pay.

So come out to Telford and see us,
you may not have been here, before,
in the fresh air of beautiful Shropshire,
just along the new M54.

And when you have finished your shopping,
what joy you'll have found, whilst your seeking,
the friendliest people you ever could meet,
who are known as "All Friends Round the Wrekin".

"The Tale of Sam and his Pigeons"

On a hillside o'erlooking the Cockshutt,
there once lived a Mon of few words,
who lived for his beer and his baccy,
his bed and his bets and his birds

His pigeons had won all the races,
from France and from Spain and elsewhere,
So often had they crossed the Channel,
they knew their way blindfolded there.

Now Sam loved his birds with a passion,
that nothing could possibly quench,
He'd watch them for hours in his garden,
while having a smoke on his bench.

It got so, that he understood them,
and learned pigeon English by heart,
while they being good sporting pigeons,
spoke best Oakengates for their part.

'Twere lovely to hear them discussing,
the many affairs of the loft,
sometimes they were shouting and squawking,
but mostly they talked nice and soft.

Every morning Owd Sam would address them,
"Good morning, my friends" he would say,
"I hope that theest all slept right soundly,
and ready to fly well today".

At which they would joyfully chorus,
"Thanks Sam, for thee good morning wish,
now be a good Mon, if thee wut now,
and put some more corn in our dish".

Then into the air they'd go soaring,
o'er Donnington, Hadley and Trench,
while Sam just sat smoking his baccy,
and taking his ease on his bench.

They'd wheel around Ketley and Wombridge,
and swoop down across Priorslee,
round the Nabb and St. Georges, and Snedshill,
until it was time for their tea.

As they came into land Sam was waiting,
to greet every pigeon by name,
He'd Christened each bird as a baby,
and no bird was ere named the same.

There was Charlie and Flossie, and William,
Rebecca and Ruby and Ted,
Young Benjamin, Isaac and Harry,
and Doris and Betty and Fred.

Ebeneezer and Lotti, and Eli,
And Margery, Elsie and Zoe,
not to mention Owd Enoch, the father,
Of Jonathon, Joby and Joe.

When Sam sent 'em off on a race day,
He'd whisper in each pigeon's ear,
"Do thee best for us wut, me owd jockey,
let's try and bring cup home, this year".

And when it was time for homecoming,
Owd Sam would be searching the sky,
for the first sight of one of his pigeons,
a sight that would gladden his eye.

As birds circled round, prior to landing,
Owd Sam would implore his small flock,
to cut out the fine aerobatics,
and get their feet down near his clock.

They usually managed to do this,
And many's the race Owd Sam won,
because he had trained all his flyers,
To come in, once race had been run.

But one day, to Owd Sam's amazement,
Young Charlie, whom he had thought soft,
had flown home from Spain, like a rocket,
and was hovering, there, above loft.

"If only he'd drop in", Sam muttered,
"He's got all the other birds skint,
this race is worth over five hundred,
for breeding, he'll be worth a mint".

Sam got on his knees to young Charlie,
and pleaded with him to come down,
but Charlie just took on him, soft like,
And circled around and around.

Then Sam lost his temper, completely,
and started to shout "Look at me,
if thee doesna come down in a minute,
Theet be in a pie for my tea".

"I canna think whatever ails thee,
thee asna done this trick, afore,
now come down at once, me owd sparrow,
about this, we'll then say no more".

ALW

But Charlie continued to circle,
and then, as though Owd Sam to tease,
flew right down to where Sam was standing,
and said, "I've got cramp in my knees".

"Thee'l have to arrange a safe landing,
on something remarkably soft,
me landing gear's gone for a burton,
that's why I can't land on thee loft".

In a flash , Owd Sam fetched out a mattress,
and shouted to Charlie, "Okay,
now let's have a nice three point landing,
to round off a wonderful day".

So Charlie went round in a circle,
and then with a consumate ease,
became the first bird to win Trophy,
by landing, with cramp in his knees.

Owd Sam were so proud of young Charlie,
he carried him round, shoulder high,
and loudly extolled his performance,
to anyone, just passing by.

So if thee sists a mon with a pigeon,
in Oakengates, Hadley or Trench,
remember the tale of Young Charlie,
Owd Sam and his garden, and bench.

*   *   *   *

A Tale of the Talents

A Circus clown of high repute,
and well known artistry,
made up his mind to be a monk,
and join a monastery.

The Abbot said "You're welcome, Son,
I don't know what you'll do,
of one thing, though, you can be sure,
We'll make a monk of you".

The Tumbler, weary of the world,
that he had left behind,
applied himself with all his might,
to work of every kind.

To please the monks, in every job,
the smoothest and the rough,
he did his best, but for the monks,
this was not good enough.

They could not seem to understand,
his inability,
to carry out the simplest chores,
to their conformity.

And so the Tumbler in a fit,
of sheer despondency,
was noted by the Bretheren to
commit a heresy.

Or so they thought, for was he not,
performing, as of old
beneath their sacred Crucifix,
of purest inlaid gold.

They fetched the Abbot; "Sir", they said,
"This Tumbler now must go,
you surely cannot keep him after,
this unseemly show".

The Holy Father watched his act,
and noted all the skill,
with which the little acrobat,
each movement would fulfill.

"You are mistaken, Brother Monks,
this is no heresy,
he's giving of his best to God,
the same as you and me".

"And though he's tried his very best,
to earn his daily bread,
because he's failed at every task,
he's doing this instead",

"For all of us have differing skills,
each one to his accord,
to place before, in simple faith,
Our Master, Friend and Lord".

ALW

"Sam........the Night Watchman"

AT beginning of war, Bank of England,
had moved Nation's bullion away,
to a place very quiet and secluded,
in Midlands, or so people say.

Some said it were somewhere in Shropshire,
While others said it were in Wales,
O'course as so happens in wartime,
there were plenty of rumours and tales.

In fact, just a few Civil Servants,
Sir Winston, and those just at hand,
were aware it had moved to a quarry,
which normally quarried for sand.

Now some of the locals round Dawley,
had reason their old eyes to doubt,
watching sand being taken to quarry,
instead of it being brought out.

One of these were Owd Sam, the night watchman,
who wanted to know more and more,
why sand being brought in were guarded,
by searchlights and sentries galore.

To add to Owd Samuel's amazement,
they stored all the sand bags on racks,
till Sam could resist it no longer,
He'd got to find riddle of sacks.

One day as a lorry were passing,
his hut, where he kept out of cold,
a sand bag fell out on the roadway,
revealing a sackful of gold.

At first Sam thought he would report it,
And claim a substantial reward,
but then he thought, "Blow it, why should I?,
that's something I can't quite afford".

"If I could get more of this lolly,
I'd chuck up this night watchman's lark,
it's not very good for rheumatics,
besides which, I don't like the dark".

So Sam made a hole in the roadway,
just close by his hut, in the road,
and each time a lorry passed o'er it,
a sand bag would fall from it's load.

Quick as light, Sam would rescue the bullion,
and bury it under the earth,
till one day he'd got so much money,
he didn't know what what he were worth.

And then the War ended, abruptly,
and Sam had to run for his life,
'cos Bankers had counted the sandbags,
and found they were one or two light.

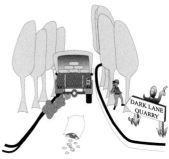

To escape from the vengeance of justice,
Owd Sam wandered all o'er the earth,
and settled in Western Australia,
in th'outback, twixt Darwin and Perth.

For twenty-eight years he remained there,
in sunshine and heat and in cold,
and then when he thought it were prudent,
he came home to look for his gold.

He arrived at Heathrow, just on tea-time,
and passed through the Customs, O.K,
but then, as he reaoned, who'd know him?,
After so many long years away.

Being lucky, Owd Sam got to Euston,
to see his train standing on line,
which meant, that if service ran promptly,
he'd reach Oakengattes about nine.

As it happened, the train were a good'un,
and steamed along nicely all way,
stopping three times before Wolverhampton,
where Local were standing in bay

For by now Sam were getting excited,
while thinking of meeting his mates,
and jumped from the train like a youngster,
when it finally reached Oakengates.

Now as Sam gave Collector his ticket,
he'd only one thing on his mind,
to nip across sharply to Public,
and down a few pints before time.

So Sam made his way to the Calé,
and drew up a stool to the bar,
while Landlord drew pint of best bitter,
and said, "Are you travelling far?".

"Oh no", said Owd Sam, only local,
about half a mile from Priorslee,
quite close to the Chapel at Dark Lane,
near quarry, below Malinslee".

Landlord looked at Owd Sam very queerly,
and said in his kindliest way,
"If your looking for Methodist Chapel,
I don't think there's one there, today",

"For over Dark Lane they've built Sainsbury's,
the place you once loved is no more,
while old Malinslee's gone forever,
replaced by a large Asda Store.

Owd Sam sat agast while he listened,
and then plucked up courage to say,
"I can hardly believe what thee tellst me,
is quarry still working today?".

" Lor bless my soul, no", said the landlord,
"They filled in the quarry, you see.
to make it the centre of Telford,
Near fountain, close by   M.E.B.".

"They tell me the land fetched a fortune,
worth it's weight, so they say, in pure gold,
and to think afore War, half an acre,
would go for a few pounds, when sold".

Owd Sam nodded weakly, and pondered,
the wisdom he often been told,
of the misery that follows the seeker,
of money and riches, and gold.

*   *   *   *

"St. Georges"

HAVE you ever stopped to wonder,
how St. Georges got it's name,
and why it's far from easy,
to find out from whence it came.

After all, it's not that common,
and there must be many, who,
would like to know it's origin,
the same as me and you.

So bearing this in mind, I thought,
I'll go and see Owd Mose,
he's bound to know St. Georges,
 and of how the name arose.

Cos this mon's lived here all his life,
from boyhood through to man,
if any one can put me right,
I'm sure Owd Moses can.

ALW

"Now sit thee down, and make theeself
at home", he said to me,
"Afore we start I'll get the wife,
to brew us up some tea".

"It's ages since I saw thee, but,
thee still looks just the same",
I replied "I've come to ask thee
how St.Georges got it's name".

Owd Moses sat and thought a bit,
then said, "I'll tell thee what,
thee come along and I'll show thee,
a certain famous spot".

"Where many years ago, before
St. Georges got it's name,
there lived a fearsome dragon,
who was difficult to tame".

Until a strapping youth, called George,
drank deeply from his flagon,
and said, "Hand down me trusty spear,
I'll fight this pesky dragon".

And that's how George, the dragon slew,
while thousands watched in fear.
between the Cockshutt and the Nabb,
right on this spot, just here.

Of course, as all the World now knows,
accomplishing this mission,
earned George the title of a Saint,
in grateful recognition.

And so when strangers asked if beast,
was still about in business,
the locals proudly said "No Sir,
but you can see.......St. George is".

Thus reassured, they said, "Well now,
we know the situation,
For evermore we must record,
this wonderful location.

"Of where young George, the dragon slew,
to end his beastly orgies,
and thus create the pleasant town,
we now know as.......St. Georges.

The trip, by the way, was to London,
a popular Tripper's request,
especially as down at the Commons,
they'd be Baldwin Webb's honoured guests

As the trains thundered through Wolverhampton,
and Birmingham, Stratford and Slough,
there were many who thought the speed frightening,
as were normally used to a plough.

And then they roared into the Station,
to Paddington G.W.R.,
the pride of the Great Western Railway,
and biggest place they'd seen, so far,

Now just outside Paddington Station,
up Praed Street, a very short way,
a famous Pub stands on the corner,
you'll have heard of it, p'raps, "Load of Hay".

Well, most of the trippers from Shropshire,
by this time, had worked up a thirst,
and thought they'd see London much better,
by downing a pint or two, first.

So while some were making for subways,
or trying to find "Waterloo",
Owd Sam and a few from "The Lion",
were soon supping best local brew.

And then it were Sam's turn to order,
so, hailing a buxom barmaid,
Owd Sam, in his very best Shropshire,
Said, "Owse gooing on, me owd blade?".

"Could'st thee fill these glasses with bitter,
we've come up from Shropshire, thee see,
and whilst theest about it, thee have one,
thee could'st have what thee likes, it's on me".

The barmaid , a lovely young Cockney,
said "Blimey, you're speaking Morse Code,
there's one thing for certain, and that is,
you're not from the dear Old Kent Road".

Now Sam and the lads kept on drinking,
with most of 'em still on their feet,
till Landlord put towels on the beer pumps,
and turned 'em all out on the street.

Owd Sam then accosted a local,
"Dost thee know the way to the Zoo?",
the Londoner thought, "He's a Frenchman",
and quickly said, "No parley-vous".

So into the City they wandered,
as happy as they'd ever been,
stopping only to spend a quick penny,
and sing once again "Nellie Dean".

They strolled all around Piccadilly,
up Bond Street, and through Leicester Square,
and when they saw Buckingham Palace,
Owd Sam said, "Thee know'st who lives there".

"I'd cut off my right hand to see her",
and just as he said that, the Queen,
appeared at a large upper window,
and made sure that she was well seen.

Owd Sam, who was full of Dutch Courage,
recalled that the fair loved the brave,
so Sam started up National Anthem,
and Queen gave him lovely big wave.

And ordered a flunkey to fetch him,
in order that she could confer,
a suitable Order or Title,
on Sam, for his singing to her.

As Sam made his way to the Palace,
he said, "Can I bring in me mates?"
"I rather think not", said the flunkey,
"They'll have to remain at the gates".

ALW

So Sam walked along the red carpet,
to talk to the Queen on her throne,
and thought it would be a nice gesture
to ask her to visit his home.

"The Tale of Snoopy"

When Les and Edna Phillips bought,
a Guest House by the sea,
they little thought the family cat,
would not delighted be.

For very few can ere resist,
the lure of Blackpool's air,
it's wondrous Tower and Promenades,
and pleasure Beach and Fair.

But though young Snoopy did his best,
to try and settle down,
his thoughts kept wandering to his
former haunts in Telford Town.

He well recalled that Famous Puss,
from Whittington who'd been,
the hero of that mighty walk,
to see Great Britain's Queen.

And so young snoopy thought, "If he
could walk from Oswestry,
in those big boots to London Town,
there must be hope for me".

"To walk the hundred miles or so,
back to my former home,
at Ketley Bank, in Shropshire, where,
I used to live and roam".

So having made his mind up, and,
convinced that he was right,
our little Shropshire moggie,
slipped away into the night.

At first, the little pussy thought
He'd go back through St. Annes,
where Ernie's winning numbers, have
changed many people's plans.

But then he thought, the Preston Road,
would equally be near,
especially as he then could see,
the famous Wigan Pier.

He wandered down through Warrington,
and soon reached Tarporley ,
where to his joy, he spied a sign,
"To Whitchurch 23".

So pressing on, though tired and sore,
but still gritting his teeth,
our feline hero found he'd reached,
the outskirts of Prees Heath.

And at that well known watering hole,
known as the Raven Inn,
poor Snoopy, on his knees by now,
was tempted to give in.

A friendly pat, a glass of milk,
which some kind person bought,
and then our puss was on his way,
to Sambrook and Newport.

Along the road to Lilleshall,
and past the C.O.D.
then through the Trench, he struggled on,
as game as game could be.

Until he saw a signpost that
made everything worthwhile,
"To Greyhound Island, Ketley Bank,
exactly half a mile".

And Snoopy knew that he had reached,
the home that he was seeking,
to be once more with all his feline,
"Friends Around the Wrekin".

A Tale of Dudley Zoo

A young man who was on the dole,
and wondering what to do,
was told a job was going at
the famous Dudley Zoo.

He wasn't too particular,
he hadn't worked for ages,
and so he gladly took the job
of cleaning out the cages.

There was a rule he must obey,
as detailed in each cage,
any damage done would be,
recovered from his wage.

His first job in the aviary proved,
to be a proper cinch,
but then his broom caught on a perch,
and killed a little finch.

He scanned the chart and found the finch,
would cost him five pounds ten,
"I can't pay that" he thought, "I'll throw
him in the lion's den.".

He then went to the monkey house,
but once again he found,
his luck was out, for now he'd knocked
a small chimp to the ground.

He noted that a chimpanzee
would cost him nine pounds ten,
so, as before, he threw the chimp,
into the lion's den.

Well, everything was going fine,
when shaking at the knees,
the young man inadvertently
upset a hive of bees.

"Oh dear", he thought "What shall I do?",
as scattered on the floor,
and crushed beneath the fallen hive,
were three score bees or more.

"I must get rid of them " he thought,
"But how and where, and when?",
and then he thought "Of course, they must
go in the lion's den"

A lion who had just arrived,
said "Do not think me rude,
but what's it like in Dudley Zoo,
especially the food?".

The other lions said "They're trying
very hard to please,
today they've served up finch and chimps,
and even mushy bees".

"The only thing that's missing, and
we think irregular,
is why with finch and chimps,
we have no salt and vinegar".

DUDLEY ZOO

ALW

82

The first part of this little monologue is very well-known, and I am grateful to the Author for the pleasure it has given me. I felt, however, that it needed a moral, for an ending, hence it's title :-

"A FRIEND INDEED"

One evening last October,
when I was far from sober,
to keep my feet from wandering I tried,
my poor legs were all a-flutter,
as I lay down in the gutter,
when a pig came up and lay down,
by my side.

We sang, "Never mind the weather,
just as long as we're together",
'till a lady passing by was heard to say,
"You can tell a man who boozes,
by the company he chooses",
so the pig got up, and slowly walked away.

There's a moral in this story,
which is plain for all to see,
if you cannot hold your liquor, when in Town,
grab the railings or a lampost,
or a passing constable,
but what'ere you do, stay upright,
don't lay down.

Then should a comrade join you,
For a merry carousel,
you can face the world together, and indeed,
prove to all, the well-known saying,
which has stood the test of time,
"That a friend in time of need's,

***** A Friend Indeed *****

"SAM and ELSIE"

OWD Sam and his wife were devoted,
as only a couple can be,
who married each other as sweethearts,
at Dawley in 1903.

Every morning he'd take her a cuppa,
and as he sat down on the bed,
She'd say, "Theest a wonderful husband",
And plant a kiss on his bald head.

One day they were talking together,
of life, after someone has died,
and Sam and his wife both agreed that,
They'd ask to be trasmogrified.

Which means, they'd return to this planet,
in the form of a fowl or a fish,
a dog or a cat or a budgie,
according to their special wish.

Now Sam's wife, whose first name was Elsie,
said, "Sam , we must think of a sign,
if thee shouldst die first, then I'll know thee,
if I shouldst go, theelt know I'm thine".

"Good Idea", said Owd Samuel, "Let's think now,
suppose we come back as a cat,
we could sleep on the bed, which is better,
than having to kip on the mat".

"And just to make sure that we're certain,
our partner is genuine, dear,
whoever returns must remember,
to nibble the other one's ear".

So having agreed on their future,
there wasn't much else they could do,
and then after getting his feet wet,
Owd Samuel developed the flu.

And though Elsie stayed up and nursed him,
the poor fellow soon passed away,
but just ere he went, he said, "Elsie,
remember, I'll come back one day".

Well, time is a wonderful healer,
and soon Elsie's tears were all dried,
she forgot about Sam and his promise,
of coming back, transmogrified.

And then she met William, a widower,
who fancied a warm comfy bed,
"You're a fine Buxom widow", he told her,
"Let's make up our minds to get wed".

So once again Elsie was settled,
as happy, as happy could be,
till one night she heard something scratching,
and went to the front door to see.

'Twas a black cat she saw on the mat, there,
and as she bent down to draw near,
she knew it was Sam in an instant,
cos Samuel was biting her ear.

When time came for bed, Sam was stationed,
on't pillow near Elsie's right ear,
"I'm not having this", said Owd William,
"That mangy cat's not staying here".

At which Elsie bridled, and told Bill,
to stop making such a to-do,
"If it comes to the crunch, this old tom-cat,
has got as much right here, as you".

So that's how they slept, until one night,
quiet peacefully, poor Elsie died,
with William asleep by her left hand,
and Sam, on the pillow beside.

As so often happens in sorrow,
to share, helps the lonely, 'tis said,
so Sam was invited by William,
to sleep with him, still, on the bed.

ALW

And thus the two husbands of Elsie,
one human, one transmogrified,
lived happily, albeit sadly,
when thinking of Elsie their "Bride"

Till one day, a lovely young she-cat,.
walked straight up to Sam, without fear,
and proved she was his darling Elsie,
by nibbling away at his ear.

Next morning, when Owd Bill awakened,
a cat lay each side of his head,
Twere Elsie and Sam, reunited,
transmogrified, there, in his bed.

ALW

*   *   *   *   *

"SAM..........and the Spacecraft"

OWD Samuel were standing near island,
      on A5, nearby Rose and Crown,
   just minding his business and thinking,
      of changes in Telford New Town.

   He thought how remarkably easy,
      a motorist possibly could,
   join ring road at Dawley or Madeley,
      and end up in Wrockwardine Wood.

   As he stood looking idly at traffic,
      he couldn't believe his old eyes,
   for out of the sky dropped an object,
      of truly remarkable size.

   It came to a halt on the island,
      adjacent to where Sam had stood,
   slap-bang in the middle of Ring-Road,
      which ends up at Wrockwardine Wood.

   The object were large flying saucer,
      from Jupiter, Venus or Mars,
   which somehow had taken wrong turning,
      while travelling around through the stars.

Now the Scots said, "Well what about Glasgow?'
we're sure this great city will do,
after all, every Saturday evening,
you sing that it *"Belongs to you"*.

The Irish considered that Derry,
with London as part of it's name,
would make a fine city, "Begorah",
and put all the others to shame.

From North and from South and from Eastward,
the M.P.'s all mooted their choice,
when up spoke the Member for Wrekin,
and said, in his best Shropshire voice.

"If theet listen to me Mr. Speaker,
I'll tell thee as much as I know,
'bout Telford and that part of Shropshire,
where London could probably go".

"You see Sir, the only things lacking,
in Telford, apart from the sea,
are one or two features of London,
which could be transferred seemingly".

"We'd soon build an "Underground" system,
the area's full of owd mines,
there'd be trains every minute from Ketley,
On Mossey Green—Oakengates Line".

"While from Donnington Wood thee cudst travel,
for tuppence or threepence a time,
to Malinslee House via Sainsbury's,
on Circle or Dawley Bank Line".

"I don't think we've got Piccadilly,
we've an Oxford Street, Regent Street, Mall,
The oldest "Iron Bridge" in the World, Sir,
and "Blists Hill Museum", as well.

"We've theatres and Churches and Chapels,
and hundreds of pubs round about,
the beer is the finest theet drink, Sir,
of that there is really no doubt.

"The Buck's Head could well be like Chelsea,
or Charlton Athletic's abode,
"Up The Hammers" would ring out o'er Sankeys,
while Arsenal could play down the road".

"You see, Mr. Speaker, we've got it,
there's no doubt that Telford's the place,
we could put Nelson's Column on't Wrekin,
with Lions as well, round the base".

"And as for the hundreds of pigeons,
which fly around Nelson, each year,
there's no need to worry on that score,
they breed, by the thousand, round here".

"I think now I've stated me case, Sir",
and M.P. for Wrekin sat down,
"You've done very well", said The Speaker,
"We'll all vote for Telford New Town".

    *   *   *   *   *

"The Saga of Evans the Pads"

THIS is the tale of a football team,
who looked like going down,
and of Mose Evans and his pals,
who lived in Telford Town.

Two of these Wolves supporters,
suffered bravely every week,
the other one, a pious man,
was what you might call meek.

Instead of ranting at the Ref.,
the linesman and the players,
this gentle, Kind, unusual man,
would quietly say his prayers.

It will not come as a surprise,
to those who knew old Moses,
to realize this weekly chore,
was not a "Bed of Roses".

For though he prayed with all his might,
and with such seeming ease,
the cold would come up from the floor,
and strike him through his knees.

Because of this the poor chap,
couldn't really concentrate,
and so his team, The Wanderers,
became quite second rate.

Things got so bad, old Moses said,
"I've got to have some knee pads,
I don't care where you get them from,
just get them to me quick, lads".

To save the famous "Wanderers",
they searched both high and low,
wherever knee pads could be found,
those lads were sure to go.

The search became their goal in life,
they searched all day and night,
until, at last with joy they spied,
a most rewarding sight.

You'll never guess, but perhaps you will,
"Hoorah" for those two lads,
at last, they found a gardener,
who was wearing two knee pads.

"Excuse us, Sir", they both chirped up,
"Can we have words with you?",
"Why surely lads, now tell me, please,
what can I do for you?".

"We'd like to buy your knee pads, Sir,
to help our team and players",
and so they told him of old Mose,
and of his mighty prayers.

The gardener aquiesed at once,
"Please take them now", quoth he,
"For such a very worthy cause,
you have my sympathy".

So Moses Evans wore the pads,
and Wolves began to win,
it was indeed uncanny,
how the Wanderers knocked 'em in.

In years to come, it shall be writ,
in letters large and bold,
of Moses Evans and his pads,
and of the "Black and Gold".

How, by his mighty praying,
The Wolves had such a run,
which took them from the "Danger Zone",
Right through Division One.

Of how they won the F.A. Cup,
and of the scene at Wembley,
when Moses shewed his knee pads,
to that wonderful assembly.

And how the Queen, God Bless Her,
looking regally so gallant,
said "Moses, Bless my Soul,
I don't know where you get your talent".

"As Baron Knee Pad Evans,
from henceforth, you shall be known,
in Oakengates, the Freedom of
The Town is now your own".

"For nowhere else in all my realm,
have I found such a man,
as Moses Evans, Preacher, Friend,
and perfect Gentleman".

Mose looked up at Her Majesty,
and said, "You've done me fine,
I've only done all this to help,
two dear old friends of mine".

'I couldn't bear to see them,
looking so depressed and sad,
when Wolverhampton Wanderers,
were having it so bad",

ALW

Her majesty said, "Were're impressed,
We'll grant by Royal Decree,
The "Order of the Knee Pad Royal",
to each of you loyal three".

"In order that my peoples, may,
when things are looking bad,
remember Moses Evans,
and the saga of his pads".

"And take such comfort as they can,
when ill befalls our Race,
of how this proud Salopian,
found such Amazing Grace".

*   *   *   *   *

"On the Buses"

IT doesn't seem that long ago,
with little or no fuss,
you could with seeming ease, ride on,
your local favourite bus.

The driver, as a rule, would be,
a Harry, Dick or Tom,
who'd recognise you instantly,
the moment you got on.

"Come on Owd Mon, let's help thee up,
and get thee in thee seat,
what's want, a single to the 'Gates,
get off at Oxford Street?".

You'd know each bus along the route,
because of it's own name,
and never have to wait for long,
before one of them came.

Like Coopers, Prices, Ashleys, Browns,
Elcocks, Hoggins, Jones and,
Martlews, which are but few,
familiar names we've known.

Each bus would take the shortest route,
between each destination,
thus making for the ultimate,
in Customer Relations.

Until the day the Midland Red,
said they would try and sell us,
a bus service for every one,
in Telford, known as Tellus.

But strange things happened from the start,
of Tellus's inception,
the buses didn't seem to go.,
in any one direction.

One bus set out for Madeley, but,
to date, has not been seen,
'twas last reported, so we're told,
somewhere near Mossey Green.

Then people on a Dawley bus,
were last seen waving madly,
as round and round they circled,
on the new ring road at Hadley.

Whilst on the best authority,
'tis said, a bus, northbound,
was last seen heading up M6,
and has not yet been found.

So in despair, Telfordians,
got up a big petition,
imploring Midland Red to re-
examine the position.

And so restore a bus service,
of which they could be jealous,
and rightly sing the praises of
their Telford Town's own Tellus.

ALW

'Tis good then to report that Tellus,
didn't make a song,
but quickly set about to find out,
what was going wrong.

Now Sam was a kind-hearted person,
and thought it would be of some note,
if he could repay all their kindness,
in taking his household to vote.

So when Polling Clerk gave him paper,
and told him to put down his cross,
Sam moved over slowly to poll-booth,
and seemed to be quite at a loss.

"If I vote for the Tory", he muttered,
"Then Labour Mon wunna get in,
and Liberal Mon seemed such a nice bloke,
Oh Dear!, what a pickle I'm in".

Then Sam had a great inspiration,
"These three have been so good to me,
instead of just voting for one one Mon,
I'll jolly well vote for all three".

When names of elected were published,
and Sam knew who was his M.P.,
he couldn't help laughing his head off,
for he'd forecast one out of three.

And to round off this wonderful story,
which not many people have heard,
he not only forecast the winner,
but also the second and third.

*   *   *   *   *

SAM.........AND THE TRAVELLER

A weary traveller from the East,
or was it p'raps the West,
drove into Telford, looking for
a place where he could rest.

He thought "I'll have to ask someone,
where I can find a pub,
which serves the finest bitter,
and a meal of homely grub".

So, stopping by a dear old soul,
who happened to be Sam,
he said "Excuse me Sir, I'm not
too certain where I am".

"Perhaps you could direct me to
a local hostelry,
where I can get a drink, and feel
that I shall welcome be".

Owd Sam thought for a minute, then,
said "If theest got a thirst,
we'd better try 'em one by one,
now which pub is the first?".

"Well, as we're up at Ketley Bank,
we haven't far to go,
let's try one in the Lord Hill bar,
a pint?, I wont say no".

"The Stafford Arms is our next call,
it's only down the street,
a double whiskey?, thankee Sir,
I think I'll try it neat".

"The Greyhound is just down the road,
and then The Rose and Crown,
another bitter?, half a mo,
I'll just drink this one down".

"The Compasses at Beveley,
the famous old White Lion,
must not be missed, because thee sist,
they're pubs thee cost rely on".

"The Unicorn, The Seven Stars,
another pint for me,
The Pear Tree Bridge and Omnibus,
are all pubs thee shouldst see".

"The Caledonian Hotel,
is famous for it's ale,
The Black Horse and The Duke of York,
thee must see without fail".

98

"The Fighting Cocks, The Elephant,
The Bush, The Bird in Hand,
The White Horse and The Albion,
are known throughout the land".

"Of course, that's only just a few,
of all the pubs round here,
why thankee Sir, theet very kind,
I'll have another beer".

"Now let me see, where was I now,
did I forget The George,
and all the many pubs around
the famous Severn Gorge?".

"The Golden Ball, The Robin Hood,
The Tontine, Valley, Crown,
together with a host of pubs,
they've recently pulled down".

ALW

"One comes to mind, without a doubt,
of special commendation,
the well-known Cuckoo Oak, alas,
became a new Fire Station".

"How good it is then to report,
they've now rebuilt this pub,
where one can still enjoy a pint,
and eat their lovely grub".

"The Beacon standing on the hill,
The Park, The Miner's Arms,
The Flags of all the Nations,
with it's special Real Ale charms".

"The Barley Mow, The Furnaces,
The Brewery, and The Boat,
that's very kind of thee, I'm sure,
a pint will ease me throat".

"We mushn't mish the old Half Moon,
The Swan, or Cheshire Cheese,
The Traveller's Joy, Labour inVain,
another bitter, please".

"The Bucksh Head, hic, The Cock Hotel,
there mush be many more,
excushe me, Shir, I really think I'm
shlipping to the floor".

"Where are we now?, jush let me think,
ish thish the Lord Hill bar?,
with all the pubs we've vishited,
we haven't got that far".

"If thee comesh't back another day,
I'll take thee round some more,
but in the meantime, Shir,
pleashe help me get up off the floor".

*   *   *   *   *

A TALE OF TELFORD UNITED

WHEN Geoff Hurst signed for Wellington,
he came on one condition,
that he would take United up
into the Fourth Division.

He looked around The Buck's Head ground,
and saw it's great potential,
but realised a well-laid pitch,
was really most essential.

So, with the Club's Directors,
who had similar ambitions,
the pitch was well prepared,
and all the turf laid in position.

United fans who well remembered
playing "Up the slope",
said "If they canna play on this,
we anna got much hope".

"Cos when thee thinks of Hedley Simms,
and players of his class,
he really would have revelled,
on this beautiful green grass".

Thus, Telford started very well,
and all seemed milk and honey,
until, out on the pitch, someone,
espied a little bunny.

The groundsman was indeed nonplussed,
as right in front of goal,
to his amazement there appeared,
a great big rabbit hole.

The ground, it seemed, was honeycombed,
with every sort of burrow,
which obviously called for action,
swift and stern and thorough.

"Inform the Press" the Chairman cried,
"We can't have these 'ere holes,
appearing in our new-laid turf,
and right in front of goal".

"Let's ask for Volunteers,
especially anyone with merit,
who'll guarantee to clear our pitch,
with dog and gun, or ferret".

The offers poured in, thick and fast,
from miles and miles around,
to clear the little bunnies,
from the famous Buck's Head ground.

The rabbits, full of Agro,
were not easily subdued,
and started chanting songs they knew,
like "We shall not be moved".

And "Whose your Father, Referee"?,
and songs in similar vein,
until the ferrets drove them up,
onto the ground, again.

It was indeed a sorry sight,
to see those Telford rabbits,
evicted from their own home ground,
because of their bad habits.

But nothing lack, they marched forthwith,
to see the Corporation,
at Priorslee Hall, and thus express,
their irate indignation.

At first, they wouldn't let them in,
then, with some hesitation,
the Chairman said "Let's play it cool,
I'll see a deputation".

And so the meeting held that day,
was something like a dream,
from which the Chairman will awake,
when he relives the scene.

For ere the meeting had begun,
the rabbits made it plain,
they would not leave, until they were
resettled, once again.

And given work in Telford, where,
they'd always felt at home,
and thus could breed like rabbits,
and so nevermore would roam.

The Chairman, a most kindly man,
on learning of their plight,
said "This is an emergency,
we must put matters right".

"It seems to me you're not the fans,
United want around,
in view of all the holes you've made
beneath the Buck's Head Ground".

He sat and thought for quite a while,
and then said with a grin,
"I think I know the very jobs
to put you rabbits in".

"The Gas Board and the M.E.B.,
are always digging holes,
The G.P.O. and Water Board
are like a lot of moles".

"I'm sure they'll welcome all of you,
to aid their excavations,
and as they seldom fill them in,
you'll have no reservations".

"So that's a Dawley Mon, thee sist,
and why I'm glad my son,
can say with pride, whenever asked,
I am a Dawley Mon".

"And why it is my fervent hope,
that when I have passed on,
St. Peter, standing at the Gates,
will say I'm glad theet come".

"For it is written, as it were,
in Heavenly manner speaking,
that now you'll join your many friends,
from all around the Wrekin".

"Who'll welcome you with open arms;
and harpsichord and song,
because to them you're 'specially
welcome. . . as a Dawley Mon".

ALW

How's Your Father

Some marriages last very long,
While others often fail,
Then fathers must pay maintenance,
or spend some time in gaol.

It was not long before young Tom
and Florrie found that they,
were incompatible, and so
would go their separate ways.

They had a lad, young Enoch, who
would live, of course, with Mum,
whilst Tom was ordered by the Court,
to pay a weekly sum.

And as Tom lived quite near, each week,
young Enoch went to Dad,
who never failed to send to Mum,
the maintenance for the lad.

Until the day arrived, at last,
when Enoch came of age,
and Tom said, "Tell your Mother, lad,
This is her final wage".

"I am no more your Father, Son,
She'll get no more from me",
When Enoch told his Mother this,
She said "Now list' to me".

"You go straight back and tell that man,
that he's been truly had,
For sixteen years he's paid for you,
but never was your Dad".

Manford's Garage, Queen's Head, Near Oswestry,
Proprietors "Manford's Bros."
Where Edward, Prince of Wales who later became King Edward VII
regularly called for petrol on his way to 'Chirk Castle'.
This Garage is still operating, but it is interesting to note in the photograph the
old time Petrol Pumps. Shell-Mex, Pratts, BP, etc.

All 'Hand Pumped' dispensing petrol at **1/6^{d} per gallon.**

The Paddington - Birkenhead Line

In the days of God's Wonderful Railway,
better known as the GWR,
one could travel all over the country,
far quicker by train than by car.

Indeed, it was such a great pleasure,
and looked upon more as a game,
to purchase a ticket to travel,
and ride on a Great Western Train.

The carriages always would sparkle,
for were they not cleaned every day,
by the staff of God's Wonderful Railway,
who worked with a will for their pay.

Punctuality first, was the order,
you could well set your watch as each train,
would promptly arrive at the station,
and leave right on time, yet again.

Whilst the staff were exceedingly helpful,
obliging and very polite,
always willing to carry one's luggage,
or from a train, help one alight.

A touch of the cap from a porter,
and "Thankee Sir, that'll do fine",
would amply repay your intention,
to tip him a sixpenny coin.

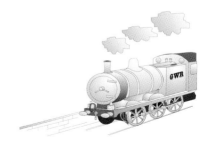

ALW

From the City of London, at Paddington,
Express trains would leave on their way,
to Merseyside via the Midlands,
returning the very same day.

What a joy to recall the announcer,
"The train leaving Platform Eleven,
is the Torbay Express, bound for Plymouth,
in the beautiful County of Devon"

"And the 9:30 Pullman for Chester,
will be calling at Leamington Spa,
Wolverhampton and Shrewsbury and Wrexham,
for passengers travelling that far"!.

These were the trains of the Thirties,
and Fourties, until British Rail,
were awarded the Government franchise,
which prompted this nostalgic tale.

For now it's a fact that the County,
of Shropshire will no longer be,
Inter-City train serviced from Euston,
and so, all Salopians agree.

That B.R..must listen and ponder,
the wishes of all who are seeking,
A through service, daily, to London, return,
for "All Friends who live 'round the Wrekin".

ALW

MOSE

One of my greatest friends was Moses Evans, who sadly, passed away in August, 1986. A real Shropshire "Character", and proud Salopian. Mose as he was affectionately known, was loved and respected by all who came under his spell.

There must be, many like myself, who still cannot believe that we shan't meet Mose, in Oakengates; coming forward, hand outstretched with his usual welcome of "Owse gooin' on, Owd Jockey?".

A prolific writer, Mose lived by, and often quoted these famous words by Abraham Lincoln.

"With Malice towards None,
With Charity for All,
With Firmness in the Right,
As God gives us to see the Right".

THE CRUCIFIX

Visitors to Hill Top Methodist Church, Ketley Bank, could, one suppose, be forgiven for wondering why a beautiful Crucifix is mounted below the pulpit. For whoever heard of a Crucifix in a Methodist Church?; There is a very simple and moving answer.

Many years ago, my Mother was passing a house, and she noticed that on top of a heap of rubbish, put out for the dustcart, was a Crucifix.

Thinking it may have been discarded by mistake, my Mother asked the householder whether this was so.
"I have no use for it" said the lady, whereupon my Mother enquired if she might have it. "Yes, take it if you like", was the reply.

I brought this to the notice of my friends at Hill Top, who agreed that the Crucifix should be restored, consecrated, and hung below the pulpit.

It has, of course, had it's critics, but to Hill Top, it is a much loved symbol of the need for tolerance and co-operation and understanding in the Church.

*　　　*　　　*　　　*　　　*

The occasion was the dinner at Oakengates Town Hall, for the last social event of the old Oakengates U.D.C. My companion diner introduced himself as Father Marmion. As we conversed, I mentioned that at my Church, many preachers took our services, but not a Catholic Priest. He said that he would love to come and talk to us. He took the evening Service on St. Patrick's Day. Afterwards, he said "I do hope you ask me here again, but tell me, do they always sing like this?" I assured him that this was so.

"I must tell my flock of the wonderful singing, here", he replied. What a compliment. He visited Hill Top again and made may friends, who still fondly remember him. He knew he was among friends; the Crucifix below the pulpit told him that, the moment he saw it. And yet, it had been thrown away with the rubbish.

Surely, the Lord works in a mysterious way, His wonders to perform.

*　　　*　　　*　　　*　　　*

Hands Around the Wrekin

Way back in 1981,
a Telford journalist,
sat looking out o'er Ketley Town,
and wondering what he'd missed.

He'd covered all the Births and Deaths,
and sundry traffic fines,
especially those who'd parked their cars,
on double yellow lines.

He thought "If only I could find
a real exclusive scoop,
the Telford Journal editor,
would be quite cock-a-hoop.

And then from somewhere fairly near,
most likely Ketley Sands,
he recognised a well-known tune,
Max Bygraves' "You need Hands".

ALW

"That's it", he thought, If all the folk
could round the Wrekin stand,
a chain of friendship would be formed,
by simply joining hands".

The Editor was thrilled to bits,
the scheme got under way,
and very few Salopians,
will 'ere forget the day.

When seventeen thousand Shropshire folk,
in nineteen eighty-one,
turned Monday, May the fourth, into
a super day of fun.

By circling round the Wrekin, in
a massive human chain,
in order that for evermore,
they could with pride, proclaim.

That on that famous day of yore,
the friendship they were seeking,
was found by young and old alike,
with "Hands Around the Wrekin".

A Recipe for Living

Many years ago, a good friend and neighbour, Mr Jack Fox of Ketley Bank, gave me his "Recipe for Living", based on Hymn number 504 in the Methodist Hymn Book. Sung to the tune "Melita", these words are an inspiration to us all.

Leave God to order all thy ways,
And hope in Him whate'er betide;
Thou'lt find Him in the evil days,
Thy all-sufficient strength and guide:
Who trusts in God's unchanging love,
Builds on the rock that nought can move.

Only thy restless heart keep still,
And wait in cheerful hope, content,
To take what'ere His gracious will,
His all-discerning love, has sent,
Nor doubt our inmost wants are known,
To Him who chose us for His own.

Sing, pray, and swerve not from His ways,
But do thine own part faithfully;
Trust His rich promises of grace,
So they shall be fulfilled in thee:
God never yet forsook at need,
The soul that trusted Him indeed.

A Proud Salopian

A Shropshire Lad once asked his Dad
in casual conversation,
why Proud Salopians had earned
this well-known reputation.

His Father said Well, first of all,
let's look at Robert Clive,
who helped to found an Empire
by his vision and his drive"

"And Mary Webb. The novelist,
and Housman, come to mind,
for literary efforts
of a most enduring kind".

"Then Captain Webb of Dawley, swam
the English Channel, and
was greeted on his homecoming
by Dawley Silver Band".

ALW

"And cheered by thousands in the streets,
who carried him on high,
to see the famous Dawley pig,
who watched the band go by".

"A column, proud, to General Hill,
reminds the County town,
of services to King and State,
for which he was renowned".

"While Darby in his famous forge
at Coalbrookdale, unfurled,
his plans to cast a bridge of iron,
the first one in the world".

"From Whitchurch, Edward German wrote,
with confidence supreme,
of "Merrie England", based, no doubt,
on Shropshire's lovely scene".

"Then Gordon Richard's great career
was crowned by royal acclaim,
with Pinza's splendid Derby win
of such immortal fame".

"In soccer, Madeley's Billy Wright,
enhanced the football scene,
as Captain of the mighty Wolves,
and of the England team".

"Nor can we 'ere forget the part
that Johnny Hancocks played,
when Wolves took on the very best
that Europe could parade".

"Bob Price of Shifnal, loved by all
who came beneath his spell,
and Percy Thrower, gardeners both,
who served their County well".

"Len Murray of the T.U.C.,
would be the first to claim,
he's still at heart a Shropshire Lad,
and proud of Shropshire's name".

"Whilst on the Fairway and the Green,
Wem scholar, Sandy Lyle,
from Hawkstone Park, has shewn the world
the way to win in style".

"These are but just a few, my Son,
who well performed their task,
and who should be remembered, when,
like you, your children, ask . . .".

"The question that you put to me,
of why Salopians Proud,
the whole world o'er are known as such,
and always thus endowed".

"And why when'ere Salopians meet,
you'll always hear them speaking,
with fond affection of their many
Friends Around the Wrekin".

THE TALE OF PRICKLY SID

One day a little hedgehog
by the name of prickly Sid,
was quite nonplussed to find himself
trapped in a cattle grid.

His only thought on leaving home,
was courting Prickly Lil,
a female hedgehog, whom to Sid,
completely filled the bill.

It therefore came as quite a shock,
and put Sid in some doubt,
to find he'd made an entrance in,
but could not find one out.

And so it dawned on Prickly Sid,
that he was now entombed,
a prisoner in a cattle grid,
convinced that he was doomed.

But Hark !, was that a footstep?,
Sid imagined it were so,
but then he thought "If that's the case,
will it be friend or foe?".

ALW

As things turned out, it was a friend,
a certain Major Coles,
whose military training,
always made him look down holes.

"Well, Bless my soul", the Major said,
"You're lucky I passed by,
because it's clear you would have starved,
and then most likely die".

"But don't despair, my little friend,
for I'll soon get you out,
in order that you can return,
to what you were about".

"And furthermore I'll tell the world,
and make a valiant bid,
to make sure there are exits built
in every cattle grid".

Young Sid was overcome with joy,
and spread the news about,
how Major Coles had spotted him,
and how he'd pulled him out.

And how this Proud Salopian
had proved to one and all,
that everyone can try and help
God's creatures, great and small.

*   *   *   *   *

HAVE A GO

When Adam got the message
that his living he must earn,
he found a lack of confidence
at every single turn.

"You'll never do it, Lad", they said,
"It simply can't be done,
it's far too big a job for you,
best pack it in, Old Son".

Then Tutankhamen thought that he
would build a mighty Sphinx,
but soon found out that first of all,
he had to fight the jinx.

"You'll never do it, Sire" they said,
"It simply can't be done,
it's far too big a job for you,
in Egypt's blazing sun".

Columbus, 'ere he sallied forth,
the seven seas to sail,
met all the usual people, who
informed him he would fail.

ALW

"You'll never do it, Chris, they said,
"It simply can't be done,
it's far too big a job for you,
in your small galleon".

And so it could be said, of all
the famous folk of yore,
who gave their best to try and do
that little something more.

From he who set his foot upon
the moon in outer space,
or bravely reached Antartica
to find and build a base.

Or seek a cure, compose a tune,
or build a tower so high,
that people would look up at it,
and say "That was some guy".

Because, despite the pessimists
who whisper in your ear,
"You can't do that, it can't be done",
it can be done, that's clear.

And when you've reached your goal,
you'll find the very people who,
were telling you that you would fail,
are full of praise for you.

"We knew you'd do it, Son", they'll say,
"We knew what you could do,
perhaps you have forgotten our
encouragement to you".

"Of course you'll do it, Son", we said,
"We knew it could be done,
we knew you'd win because you are
a Proud Salopian".

A BIT OF THE BACK

As far back as could be remembered,
whenever you met poor old Jack,
he'd wish you "Good Day", and then sadly say,
"I've got a wee bit of the back".

When at school, and the rest of his classmates,
were milling around in the pack,
this youngster would say "I can't play today,
I've got a wee bit of the back".

In his teens, when it came to the quickstep,
the Charleston, or Balling the Jack,
his partner would sigh, as she sat idly by,
poor old Jack and his bit of the back

When the day came for Jack to be married,
you'd a thought he were going on't rack,
but walking down aisle, he managed to smile,
despite a wee bit of the back.

When the wedding reception reception was over,
and guests had drunk more than their whack,
they all advised Jill to remember the pill,
which Jack had to take, for his back.

The honeymoon lasted a fortnight,
and Jill was so proud of her Jack,
as over the threshold he carried her high,
despite a wee bit of the back.

At factory, whenever a workmate,
said "Give us a lift, will you, Jack?",
he say "Well I would, if I jolly well could,
but I've got a wee bit of the back".

Due to shortage of work, Firm said "Jack, Lad,
we've decided to give you the sack,
We're sure this is best, and we know that the rest,
will be good for your bit of the back".

So Jack entered into retirement,
spending most of his time at the quack,
who knew his complaint, and so with restraint,
treated Jack for his bit of the back.

As will happen to all who are living,
life gradually ended for Jack,
but still, as he lay, he managed to say,
"I've got a wee bit of the back".

And to Jill he said "When I am gone, dear,
you'll have quite a job to keep track,
of the money I've left, for the way you've put up,
with me wee little bit of the back".

*   *   *   *   *

The Author

*Born at Evesham in 1916, Jack came to Shropshire in 1932, and having
lived in this delightful County for well over 50 years, likes to think that he
can now call himself a "Proud Salopian", if only by adoption.*

THE CHRISTENING

The notice in Wellington Journal,
was easily spotted, and read,
"Grateful thanks to the Lord for the gift of,
two babies to Doris and Ted".

Of course, they were twins, as you'll gather,
and just to complete parent's joy,
the one was a sweet little girlie,
the other, a bonny big boy.

Relation and neighbours, as usual,
were quick to come up with some names,
for the twins who would shortly be christened,
at the old parish Church of St. James.

There were some who said "Call the lad, Phillip,
a Princely name that one would be",
while others preferred Zechariah,
from out of the Bible, you see.

For the little girl everyone voted,
for Lottie, or Lindy or Lou,
but Doris and Ted said "Give over,
We've thought of the names for our two".

So, just before Christening was started,
the vicar said "Doris and Ted,
Wilt give me the names of thy offspring?,
so I can annoint each one's head".

"The little girl's name will be Freda",
said Doris, and looking at Ted,
"Thee tell him the name of the t'other",
so Ted said "The boy's name is Fred".

The Vicar was just going to christen
as Frederick, the first little tot,
when Mother said "Owd up, your Reverence,
that's, Freda not Frederik, theese got".

"I can tell by the way that she's smiling,
she's taken a liking to thee",
"I can well believe that", said the Vicar,
"For by gum, she's well christened me".

"And but for thee Mother's quick thinking,
they'd all call thee Frederick or Fred,
but now I'm aware of the difference,
I'll christen thee Freda, instead".

ALW

THE DATE

A survey, once, was carried out,
to ascertain the way,
the general public classified
the things they did each day.

Some thought their daily prayers were of
the very highest mode,
whilst many others said they tried
to keep the Hihghway Code.

To help one's neighbours seemed to be
quite well up on the list,
as one could then lay claim to be
a true philanthropist.

Some answers were amusing, and
of wide variety,
but one revealed a common bond,
in our society.

It is, of course, the date we write,
and question not, nor doubt,
the reason why the date is such,
and how it came about.

The year is Anno Domini,
or, as we say, AD,
which commonly translated means
the year of Deity.

And even those professing no
belief in God's own word,
will find the date they write proclaims
the Living Risen Lord.

For is it not recorded in
that passage all sublime,
"Lo, I am with you, evermore,
until the end of time".

The Golden Wedding

A Golden Wedding is the time,
when couples celebrate,
the day that they walked down the aisle,
in blissful married state.

Thus, Sam and Elsie went to bed,
recalling fifty years,
of all their many memories,
of laughter, joy and tears.

And as they lay there, Elsie said,
"You used to hold my hand",
"I did" said Sam "It was I thought,
the sweetest in the land".

"And then" she said "You'd kiss me,
on the lips and hold me tight",
Old Sam thought "Stone the crows, shall I,
get any peace tonight?".

But Elsie, getting passionate,
recalling yesteryear,
reminded Sam of all the times,
he loved to stroke her ear.

She said "You used to bite my neck,
to prove you loved me more",
at which Sam leapt out of the bed,
and crossed the bedroom floor.

"Whatever are you doing Sam?",
said Elsie, as he went,
"I'm going to get me teeth" said Sam,
"They're in the Steradent".

Poor Elsie knew her moment of
romance had gone for good,
When Sam returned he found her fast
asleep, but understood.

AN ODE TO THE M54

As Motorways come, I suppose the M1,
could by no means be classed as a beauty,
yet thousands of motorists use it each day,
in the course of their business and duty.

Then, Motorway 2 may be just right for you,
if you're thinking of crossing the sea,
or you may well prefer an alternative route
to the coast, on the Motorway 3.

On the M25 be alert and alive,
if in one piece you want to arrive,
whilst on the M4 there are hold-ups galore,
even more than the dreaded M5.

But who can resist driving down the M6,
and finding the usual obstruction,
including a tailback of 10 miles or so,
from the aptly-named Spa-ghetti Junction?.

You may well exclaim "Are all roadways the same?",
and the answer is "Not on your Nellie,
for there is a Motorway, quiet and refined,
which is not often seen on the Tele".

It runs from the Motorway 6, through the County
of Shropshire, to Telford, and on
to the famous A5, and it's pleasurable drive
to the valleys and hillsides of song.

If you want to know more, it's the M54,
which you'll find on the map, if you're seeking,
the welcome that everyone knows they'll receive,
from the good folk who live 'round the Wrekin.

A SHROPSHIRE HUNTING TALE

Of all the many sporting names
to grace the Shropshire scene,
The Wheatland Hunt is surely held
in very high esteem.

Along and under Wenlock Edge,
with rider, horse and hound,
The Wheatland Hunt would chase the fox,
that's if he could be found.

In fact, it could be fairly said,
that once he'd got the scent,
the fox's chance of reaching home
was less than one per cent.

Except, that is, for one old fox,
who'd managed to contrive,
the laudable ambition of
continuing alive.

And though they tried to hunt him down
with all their might and main,
it had to be acknowledged, he
possessed a super brain.

The Master of the Hunt, declared
'To catch this rascal, rare,
I think we'll try the "Gentle Touch",
to lure him from his lair".

And so, at last, it was agreed
to train a female hound,
to lead the famous Wheatland pack,
and run the fox to ground.

Because, although this might appear
to be unorthodox,
it was worth trying anything,
to catch that wily fox.

For, as a woman often gains
her end, by intuition,
'twas possible a lady dog
might fox the opposition,

And so, from all o'er Wenlock Edge,
and from the Corvedale farms,
The Wheatland Hunt assembled at
the famous Gaskell Arms.

The stirrup cup was handed round,
but little did they know,
that day, they would make history,
as the following will shew.

At first, the hounds picked up the scent,
which led them out to Bourton,
but then they doubled back, through Stretton
Westwood to Callaughton.

From whence, they charged through Wenlock,
on the road which leads to Broseley,
then o'er the bridge at Coalport,
through Ironbridge, and on to Doseley.

Across the fields to Uppington,
and Eaton Constantine,
the hunt sped on but of the fox,
they didn't see a sign.

Until, the Master of the Hunt
reigned in his horse, and said,
"I'll ask this fellow by the stile
how far the pack's ahead".

"Excuse me, have you seen a fox?,
the one that we are seeking,
has led the Hunt a merry dance,
all round and round the Wrekin".

The yokel said "He's just passed by,
and though this sounds absurd,
a little bitch be leading pack,
while fox be lying third".

ONE'S PARTICULARS

In Iolanthe, Gilbert wrote,
"That each babe born alive,
would either a young Liberal be,
or a Conservative".

Thus catalogued, in infancy,
you'll find it most essential,
your name and full address to know,
as part of your credentials.

The local Registrar of Births,
will ask "Is this a lad?",
and "Can I take it, Madam,
thast this Man's the baby's dad?".

ALW

In Church, the Parson will enquire
"What is the baby's name?,
in order that I can confer
a Christian Name on same".

In school, the teacher will, each morn,
as by the law direct,
endeavour to find out if all
are present and correct.

And when, at last, your living,
in the World you have to earn,
it seems that all officialdom,
will for your details yearn.

Computers will compute your bills,
including rates and rent,
while delving into all the reasons,
why you overspent.

Until the day arrives when you
can draw the Old Age Pension,
and hope, perhaps, to live in peace,
at least, that's your intention.

Think not, however, this is now
the end of your form-filling,
as you'll discover, very soon,
it's only the beginning.

For Pensioners, it seems must fill
in forms and forms galore,
before they are entitled to
that little something more.

Until Life's race has run it's course,
and even then your name,
must be recorded on a form,
to verify the same.

Perhaps we can't help wondering, as
we see the Promised Land,
if some official Angel will
be there with pen in hand.

Approaching us, and saying with
a most angelic ease,
"I would be grateful if you'd kindly
fill this form in, please".

"You'll note, perhaps there is no
mention of your wordly wealth,
the only thing we want to know,
is that you are yourself".

"Because, you see we know full well,
from where and whence you came,
the only question on the form,
is State your Christian Name".

"In order that we can ensure,
the dear ones you are seeking,
will welcome you, as one of all
their Friends Around the Wrekin".

TELFORD CENTRAL

The Planning Staff at Priorslee Hall,
of Telford Corporation,
were full of all the joys of Spring,
and self congratulation.

For had they not achieved, at last,
their object all sublime,
a fine new railway station,
on the Shrewsbury - London Line.

A Station which would welcome folk,
who came to Telford Town,
to live and work in Shropshire's
biggest City of renown.

A Station which would surely bid,
them "Godspeed" on their way,
and hope they would return again,
to Telford Town, one day.

And so a Proud Salopian,
Sir Lionel Murray (Len),
declared the Station open,
as it's leading Citizen.

Telfordians were overjoyed,
with their new Railway station;
and ticket sales were brisk, to
every kind of destination.

ALW

From Hollinswood and Sutton Hill,
Ironbridge and Coalbrookdale,
it was indeed amazing how,
they flocked to British Rail.

'Till B.R. said "We've cracked it now,
the world can see we care,
and justify our motto, that,
at last "We're getting there".

And then, alas, t'was found that Telford
Central wouldn't do,
because the Station hadn't got
a Gents or Ladies Loo.

And as the nearest one of these
was half a mile away,
a call of nature could be
"Fait accompli", as they say.

In fact, it was quite common,
though undoubtedly a trial,
for those "Caught short" to set a
new "Loo" record for the mile.

Which could well be the reason why
B.R. went to such pains,
to advertise with so much fuss,
their local "Sprinter" trains.

T'was pointed out by British Rail,
if travellers could forebear,
they'd find a toilet on the train,
if they could "Make it there".

But news got round, as truth will out,
of all those in distress,
and how the ticket sales were now
becoming less and less.

And so, at last, B.R. agreed,
the least that they could do,
to help the travelling public,
was to quickly build a loo.

Thus making Telford Central,
a fine Station to be seeking,
when travelling to or from their
many "Friends Around the Wrekin".

"A TOUCH O' THE BRUSH"

On a hillside o'er looking the valley,
in a very well-known Shropshire town,
there once lived a most famous Doctor,
of skill, and repute, and renown.

The ethics of medical practice,
forbid me to mention his name,
but those of his patients still living,
will know who it is, just the same.

For as they queued up in the surgery,
they knew what their treatment would be,
a touch of the brush that he kept on his desk,
in a bottle of "Iodine tea".

He used the same brush for each patient,
and wrought the most wonderful cures,
from earache to acne, and goitre and gout,
his treatment was simple and sure.

Of course, as you'll gather, t'was prudent,
to ask the next one in the queue,
their reason for seeing the Doctor,
and what he would probably do.

With his brush which he wielded so deftly,
on all of his sufferers, and each,
of the various parts of their bodies,
which no other brush could e're reach.

For when his appointment had ended,
your turn would be next to go in,
and p'raps have your tonsils well tickled,
with the brush that had just tickled him.

Thus, many a long suffering patient,
on learning their neighbour's complaint,
would quickly turn pale, and in some cases fail,
to avoid going into a faint.

Their memory would be quite amazing,
"Oh dear, did I lock the front door?,
I really must fly, you'll understand why,
I must go at once, that's for sure".

Indeed, it quite puzzled the Doctor,
why so many patients were cured,
before they had even set foot in his door,
and so, as it happens, the word.

Of the Doctor's old brush became famous,
with patients from near and from far,
queueing up for a touch of the Iodine brush,
ever there, on his desk, in a jar.

And many of those who've been seeking,
relief from their misery and pain,
can join all their friends 'round the Wrekin,
in praising the good Doctor's name.

Whose wonderfull treatment will ever,
help so many people recall,
the day that they went for a touch o' the brush,
and were cured without doubt, one and all.

From the Family Album

I suppose all of us have in our possession certain old photos, which, due to their content, may be of general interest.

How many of our readers, will I wonder, recognise some very well-known names in Show Business, in this old war-time snap, taken on 2nd April, 1940.

The place, Outside our billet, 44 Sea View Parade, Morecambe, R.A.F. recruits on the square-bashing course, before being posted to our Squadrons.

Most of us were, and probably still are, the Tom, Dick and Harrys of this world, but among the group, shown below are the founder members of "The Squadronaires", one of the greatest outfits, ever, of the Big Band era.

Can you recognise them?
Jimmy Miller (Vocalist), Harry Lewis (Clarinet), who married Dame Vera Lynn, Eric Cook (Trombone), Johnny Bradbury (Sax), Jock Cummings (Drums), Ronnie Aldrich (Piano) now musical Director of the Benny Hill Show, and top right, George Chisholm (Trombone) who delighted with his many great performances on T/V.
ME? I'm next to George (2nd top right).

SAM..........AT THE DENTISTS

In the days before National Health Service,
when treatment were not on the State,
in some parts of Country 'twere common,
to ask for relief on the slate.

Thus, many a poor country doctor,
or dentist, for that matter, too,
would do all they could for a patient,
and only receive I.O.U.

So, many a poor chap would suffer,
or perhaps even go to the vet,
than turn up for treatment at surgery,
and get himself deeper in debt.

One of these were Owd Samuel from Wombridge,
who suffered a terrible lot,
but wouldn't receive any treatment,
unless he could pay on the spot.

The doctors and dentists had cured him,
of gallstones and goitre and gout,
they'd filled all his teeth with amalgam,
and whipped his appendix right out.

Then new dentist came to the district,
a man who'd be happy between,
the scrum of a rugby league outfit,
or maybe a rugger fifteen.

Now, as he were starting in business,
he thought what a good thing 'twould be,
to advertise widely the slogan,
"For one week I'll treat you all free".

For though he had done well at college,
and passed as a dentist, forsooth,
the fact is that up to the present,
he hadn't yet pulled out a tooth.

Now Sam had a rare bout of toothache,
a double tooth right at the back,
were driving him near to distraction,
like thumbscrew, or being on't rack.

So, along to the dentist he ambled,
and knocked on the door, timidly,
as we all do when we get the toothache,
and yet pretend so brave to be.

To receptionist, Sam said "Good Morning,
I've come in response to the Ad,
to have my teeth seen to for nothing,
cos one of 'ems driving me mad".

Receptionist went into surgery,
and whispered in young dentist's ear,
"I think your first patient's in passage,
with very bad toothache, I fear".

DENTISTS
SURGERY

ALW

Well, show him in then", said the dentist,
and when he'd got Sam in the chair,
he rolled up his sleeves to his elbows,
and gave him a very queer stare.

"Do you know you're my very first patient?,
I've only had dummies, you see,
so open your mouth wide and tell me,
whatever the matter can be".

Owd Sam said "It's right at the back, Sir",
so dentist said "Hang on my man",
and getting his forceps well anchored,
he pulled on Owd Sam's double fang.

Sam screamed like a baby, and pleaded
with dentist to let him off hook,
but dentist said "Not on your life, Sam,
I'm doing all this by the book".

In the struggle the chair had tipped over,
and dentist and Sam were on't floor,
with Sam screaming loudly, blue murder,
and dentist just hanging on more.

They were just like a couple of wrestlers,
with Sam's head between dentist's knees,
in a crouch and a perfect half-nelson,
as oft on the Tele one sees.

Till Sam said "Theese pulling my head off,
I'll never come near thee, again,
the least thee cos do for a patient,
is give him a shot of cocaine".

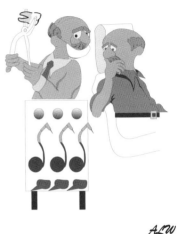

By this time the dentist were sitting,
on top of Owd Sam's hairy chest,
and though it may seem trite to say so,
Owd Sam were by no means impressed.

At last, after titanic struggle.
Sam's molar came tumbling out,
and dentist said "Yippee, I've done it,
I'm qualified now, without doubt".

ALW

"I've pulled out me very first molar,
a wonderful dentist I'll be,
said Sam "Well, if that's thy opion,
theest pulled out the last one for me".

"If thee thinkst that theest going to get me,
on't floor, owding on to my jaw,
well then, theese got another think coming,
cos I canna stand anymore".

"I don't want to knock thee profession,
I know that we've all got to eat,
but if thee takes my tip, theel sell up, lad,
and get thee a job pulling beet".

"Cos dentistry's not up thy street, lad,
it's painfully clear for to see,
there's one thing for certain, and that is,
a dentist thee never will be".

THE CUSTOM

In the days of the Great Western Railway,
from Paddington right through to Crewe,
many customs were held to be sacred,
whilst others were strictly taboo.

One custom, concerned Station Masters,
who, 'tis said, on the day they retired,
would sit at their desk in their office,
feeling lonely, dejected and tired.

Until it was time to relinquish,
the post they had held o'er the years,
and so all the Staff would assemble,
with some of them nearly in tears.

The Boss, then, as everyone knew him,
would pick up his pen on his desk,
and dipping it into the inkwell,
throw it up to the ceiling, with zest.

And then at the same time, he'd utter,
but now without sorrow or frown,
"Well, I've thrown me pen up to the ceiling,
the next Mon can get that thing down".

And so e'en today you will notice,
if you will but look up and see,
o'er the desk of the late Station Master,
where the inkspots could very well be.

Perhaps, when you're next at a station,
such as Wellington, Shrewsbury or Wem,
give a thought for the old Master's office,
his desk, and his inkwell . . .and pen.

*I am indebted to my good friend, Cecil Morris,
Ex G.W.R., for this true and delightful story.*

It is the prerogative of the National Children's Home
to confer the Distinguished Order of St. Christopher
upon members of the public, in appreciation of their
service to the work of NCH.

THIS is the LEGEND of . . . St. CHRISTOPHER

In ancient days, a mighty man,
of height and strength supreme,
would on his shoulders carry folk,
across a raging stream.

One day, as he was ferrying
a very small young boy,
he nearly stumbled and exclaimed,
"Forsooth, I know not why".

"For had I borne the whole wide world
upon my back, I vow,
there is no way it could have weighed,
as heavy child, as thou".

To which the infant thus replied,
"Oh marvel not, my Son,
Thou hast indeed bourne all the world,
and HIM from Kingdom Come".

"Henceforth, as good St. Christopher,
thy name shall ever be,
in loving recognition of
the day thou carried'st me".

And so the legend of this Saint,
which is so widely known,
is just as real when practised by
the National Children's Home.

Whose mission is to save a child,
from want and misery,
as HE commanded long ago,
in far off Galilee.

THE LAST TESTAMENT OF SAM

One day, when Enoch called on Sam,
to ask about his health,
he found him somewhat pensive-like,
and not his usual self.

"What ails thee, Sam Lad?", Enoch said,
"Thee hasna got a chill?",
"Oh no", Owd Sam said, "Actually,
I'm thinking of me will".

"Thee sist, I wouldna like to think,
that when HE calls me name,
me relatives will say Theet think
Owd Sam would play the game".

"And grumble that I hadn't left
to them, however small,
a little something, which would help
my memory to recall".

Owd Enoch said "If that's the case,
thee ought's to make a list,
exactly what theet got to leave,
so no-one will be missed".

ALW

"I'm glad theet come", Owd Sam replied,
"I know theet do thy part,
let's get the pen and paper out,
then we can make a start".

"Now Enoch, Lad, I've always known
theet fancied me false teeth,
so when I've gone, to thee, owd friend,
me dentures I bequeath".

"And though we saw not eye to eye,
to my young Brother Fred,
I gladly leave me owd glass eye,
for him to eye, instead".

"And then there is me hearing aid,
I'll pass that on to Ted,
because I'm sure he never heard
a single word I said".

"Me socks and suits and boots and shoes,
I leave to Brother Alf,
he's never seemed to have a clue,
on how to dress himself".

"The house, and all that it contains,
shall go to Brother Ben,
at least, he has come round to see
me, every now and then".

"Now let me see, I think we've gone
quite fairly through the list,
I canna think of anyone,
or anything I've missed".

"Except, that in the bank theet find
a bit of surplus cash,
I'd like a decent funeral, but
thee needsna go too rash".

"And what's left over, thee cudst have,
I wish it could be more,
especially as theest acting as
my sole executor".

Owd Enoch said "There is one thing,
on which we must agree,
and that's the wording on thy stone,
and where it is to be".

"Owd Sam replied "I care not where
my resting place will be,
providing it's in Shropshire, and
the Wrekin thee cudst see".

"As to the wording on me stone,
for when I have passed on,
Well, how about, **"HERE LIES OWD SAM,
A PROUD SALOPIAN".**

ALW

I am indebted to a very old friend, Mr Norman Martin
of Edgmond, for the following story.

MARTIN'S PERUVIAN LILY

A Sales Director thought that he
would while away the hours,
of sitting at his office desk,
by gazing at the flowers.

That he'd arranged in sundry pots,
forsooth to catch the eye,
of VIPs and customers.
Who'd call on him to buy.

One day, a member of his staff,
said "Sir, I've brought for you,
a seed as precious a pearl,
from faraway Peru".

"It came by post this morning from
a customer of ours,
whose hobby is the growing of
these rare Peruvian flowers".

"It's known as Martin's Lilly, for
a tourist of that name,
whilst seeking Desert Lillies, found
this plant of such acclaim".

"Which must be watered every day,
and tended on the hour,
in order that it can produce,
it's sweetly scented flower".

The Sales Director, overjoyed,
looked at the little seed,
and personally planted it,
and wished it all God Speed.

It was his crowning joy in life,
and soon became the talk,
of everybody in the works,
in every trade and walk.

I'll enter it in all the shows",
The Sales Director said,
and so he nursed and fed it, like
a patient, ill in bed.

Until, one day he noticed that
the apple of his eye,
resembled something he had seen
in many a Shepherd's Pie.

And so the plant turned out to be,
a common garden swede,
and not, as every body thought,
a rare Peruvian seed.

The Sales Director knew that he'd
been taken for a ride.
And gnashed his teeth, and promised that
he'd flay some rascal's hide.

Who'd led him up the garden path,
and made him look so silly,
because he thought he'd grown that most
exotic Desert Lily.

The Company was Lilleshall,
Steel Fettlers of Priorslee,
The perpetrator of the joke,
related this to me.

And with his hand upon his heart,
vouchsafed this tale was true,
The story of a common swede,
and faraway . . . Peru.

ALW

THE SHROPSHIRE STAR

Oh, twinkle, twinkle, Shropshire Star,
I often wonder where you are,
because, for reasons oft unknown,
you're not delivered to my home.

For teatime, then, is not the same,
I cannot read of last night's game,
and learn if errant Shrewsbury Town,
are staying up, or going down.

ALW

Or whether Wolves, with their tradition,
will finish top of their Division,
and whether Telford's gallant team,
will grace the Fourth Division scene.

And furthermore, I do not know,
what's on the evening radio,
or whether BBC/TV,
is preferable to ITV.

Nor, on the City page, digest,
the Shares in which I should invest,
or never fail to be impressed,
when Shirley Tart is at her best.

I could well miss a house for sale,
a bargain fare from British Rail,
or turning to the classifieds,
the latest fashion wear for brides.

I'll miss the letters in Star Mail,
although I never cease or fail
to marvel at the same old few,
who would their favourite cause pursue.

And who, or so it would appear,
write every day throughout the year,
regardless of the postage due,
to press their various points of view.

The newly hatched, and just despatched,
and wedding couples, happy matched,
This is one page I can't resist,
and never, ever, should be missed.

Whilst who could fail to sympathise,
with those who wish to form new ties,
like "Handsome Gent of sixty-one,
seeks partner for a bit of fun".

And so this plea, unorthodox,
is nightly, through my letter-box,
please drop in, like the friend you are,
our ever welcome Shropshire Star.

To cheer your many readers, who
the news and views are seeking,
of Proud Salopians, everywhere,
and "All Friends 'Round the Wrekin".

On the 12th of March, 1988, my good friend, George Raxster, and the
Telford Light Orchestra, gave their services, with other local artists
at a concert, in the Dawley Christian Centre, in aid of the Wrekin
Support Group of the National Children's Home.
This was my way of shewing the Group's appreciation.

FRIENDS of the NCH.

This is a tribute, most sincere,
to all of you who've gathered here,
The National Children's Home to cheer,
by your support throughout the year.

To you, who with collecting box,
on street collection days,
have stood for hours, come rain or shine,
that small amount to raise.

And wonder if it's really worth,
the effort you've put in,
when some folk even cross the street,
to miss your little tin.

Or on a doorstep, cold and tired,
just wondering how you'll fare,
you knock and knock, but no-one comes,
although you know they're there.

Or then again, there's just the few,
who scowl at you, and say
"Cor, stone the crows, not you again,
there's nowt for you today".

But what a difference, when, next door,
some good soul with a smile,
says "National Children's Home,
now, that's a cause that's well worthwhile".

And empties all her coppers from a purse
well worn and old,
to some folk they would not seem much,
to you, they're purest gold.

For she has now restored your faith,
you're walking ten feet tall,
The world seems such a better place,
and not that bad, at all.

And so the National Children's Home,
thanks all it's many friends,
who labour in so many ways,
Its many lives to mend.

And thanks the kindly artists, who
give of their talents, rare,
and spare the time to help a cause,
in which so many share.

The well-being and happiness,
The NCH are seeking,
for children all around the world,
and OURS around the Wrekin.

The Children's Hope House Hospice, now
requires our full support,
for by its worthy motives, much
great healing will be wrought.

In years to come, Salopians,
will thus be proud to say,
"We did our best to help the
Kiddies in this special way".

THE COUNTIES

A teacher in a Shropshire school,
said "For a bit of fun,
let's see if we can name the
English Counties, one by one".

"There's Hereford and Hertfordshire,
and Bedford, Berks and Bucks,
which boasts the town of Aylesbury,
and it's famous Aylesbury ducks".

"Oxfordshire and Cambridge, where
the colleges are found,
and Middlesex and Surrey,
with their well-known cricket grounds".

"Nottingham and Norfolk, not
forgetting Northants, too,
renowned the whole World over,
for its famous boot and shoe".

Somerset and Leicestershire,
and Cheshire, famed for cheese,
Wiltshire, York and Cornwall,
with its wonderful sea breeze".

Rutland, with its claim to be,
the smallest of them all,
and London with its Piccadilly,
Leicester Square and Mall".

Sparkling Sussex by the sea,
and Suffolk with its Shires,
Worcester, Gloucester, Durham,
and their proud Cathederal Spires".

ALW

Northumberland and Cumberland,
and Westmorland and Kent,
and in the Midlands, Staffordshire,
whose river is the Trent".

"Essex, Hunts and Lincolnshire,
and Monmouth on the Wye,
Lancashire and Blackpool,
with its famous Tower, so high".

"Derby, Dorset, Warwickshire,
whose castle is supreme,
Hants and Devon in the South,
so famous for its cream".

"Now, have we left a County out,
from those we have been seeking?,
of course, there's Shropshire, world renowned,
for "All Friends 'Round the Wrekin".

*   *   *   *   *

THE WREKIN LIGHT

The book of Genesis reveals
that on the seventh day,
The Good Lord rested from his work,
His wonders to survey.

He'd made the Earth, the Sun and Moon,
the seas, the day and night,
but first of all, the Good Book says
that God created Light.

Since when, it has been evident,
that, as in days of old,
the priceless gift of light is far,
more valuable than gold.

The Three Kings from the Orient,
Wise Men who'd travelled far,
were guided to a lowly Crib,
by following a Star.

Then, looking back to ancient times,
the lighthouse shining bright,
would warn the sailor of the many
perils of the night.

The lamp of Florence Nightingale,
would light a soldier's face,
a torch of Faith, held by an Angel
of Amazing Grace.

The miner's Davy Lamp reminds
us of the debt we owe,
to those who labour in the dark
and gloomy depths, below.

Small wonder then, in modern times,
that when a Beacon bright,
shone out across the Shropshire plain,
Salopians at night . . .

ALW

Would search the sky from North and South,
and from the East and West,
to view the famous Wrekin Light,
on Wrekin's noble crest.

The flashing beacon seemed to say,
as though a friend was speaking,
"A Shropshire welcome bids you join
All Friends Around the Wrekin".

This Monologue was first rendered at,
Hill Top Methodist Church, Ketley Bank,
At the Christmas Service, December 1983,
With the additional two verses, which,
Surely provide the perfect ending to,
This collection of Shropshire Monologues

This Christmas time we have a Light,
to guide us on our way,
The Light that shone o'er Bethlehem,
shines just as bright today.

And may the Peace and Joy this brings,
which all the world is seeking,
shine now, and evermore, on all
OUR Friends Around the Wrekin.

"All Friends Around the Wrekin" ...."Is the kind of book that any Proud Salopian would be delighted to have at home"
Shirley Tart, Shropshire Star 1987

"MORE Friends around the Wrekin" ...."Would look well on any proud Salopian's bookshelf".
Mary Queally, Shrewsbury Chronicle 1987

"EVEN More Friends Around the Wrekin"..........."Verses, memories, pouring exuberantly from Jack Insall's prolific pen".
The Right Honourable Lord Murray of Epping Forest OBE

"You Must be Joking"..."The monologues will not only keep you in stitches, but will also raise much needed funds for some of this country's most vulnerable children".
Rev. Bill Lynn, NCH Action for Children

"All Friends Around the Wrekin"......................"What a great pleasure it is for me to commend the reader to dip into the pages of this book, I warm to his wry sketches of the friendly characters who fill the pages".
Viscount Tonypandy, George Thomas
Former Speaker of the House of Commons,
and Past President of the National Children's Home

"The Best of All Friends 'Round the Wrekin"..............."Many thanks for your efforts to help Hope House in this way".
Nuala O'Kane
Appeals Director,
Hope House Children's Respite Hospice

This book is available from

Hope House Children's Hospice
Nant Lane, Morda, Nr. Oswestry, Shropshire

Hope House Appeals Office
12 English Walls, Oswestry, Shropshire

All **Hope House** Shops

Supporters of **Hope House**

or a *signed* copy from the author can be obtained – £4.99 plus 76p p&p = £5.75

Overseas £4.99 plus £1.30 p&p = £6.29

From

Mr Jack Insall
Instree, Hillside Road
Ketley Bank, Telford, Shropshire TF2 0BZ

It is anticipated that, at some future date, this book will be made available through selected bookshops for general sale.

Jack Insall
(Author and Publisher)
Tel.: 01952 612707